T V A

Democracy on the March

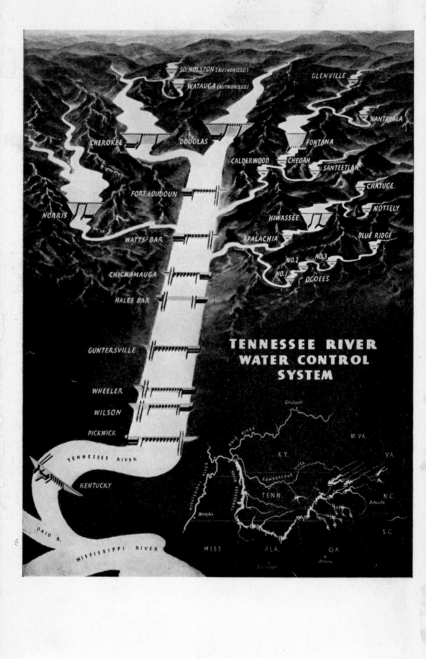

SO. HOLSTON (AUTHORIZED)
WATAUGA (AUTHORIZED)
GLENVILLE
NANTAHALA
CHEROKEE
DOUGLAS
FONTANA
CALDERWOOD
CHEOAH
SANTEETLAH
FORT LOUDOUN
CHATUGE
NOTTELY
NORRIS
HIWASSEE
BLUE RIDGE
WATTS BAR
APALACHIA
NO.2
NO.3
NO.1
OCOEES
CHICKAMAUGA
HALES BAR

TENNESSEE RIVER
WATER CONTROL
SYSTEM

GUNTERSVILLE

WHEELER
WILSON
PICKWICK

TENNESSEE RIVER

KENTUCKY

OHIO R.

MISSISSIPPI RIVER

Cincinnati

OHIO RIVER

W. VA.

K.Y.

VA.

CUMBERLAND RIVER

TENN.

N.C.

Asheville

Memphis

S.C.

MISS.

ALA.

GA.

TVA

DEMOCRACY ON THE MARCH

by

DAVID E. LILIENTHAL
Chairman, Tennessee Valley Authority

HARPER & BROTHERS PUBLISHERS

NEW YORK AND LONDON

TVA—DEMOCRACY ON THE MARCH

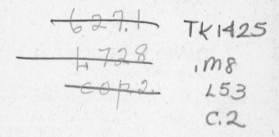

This book is complete and unabridged
in contents, and is manufactured in strict
conformity with Government regulations
for saving paper.

DEDICATED

TO

THE PEOPLE WHO LIVE IN THE

TENNESSEE VALLEY REGION

CONTENTS

vii

CONTENTS

CONTENTS

PREFACE

This is a book about tomorrow.

My purpose in writing it today is to try to cut through the fog of uncertainty and confusion about tomorrow that envelops us. The fog is caused largely by words, words without reality in the world as it actually is; to dispel this murkiness we must *see the reality behind the words.*

This book then is about real things and real people: rivers and how to develop them; new factories and new jobs and how they were created; farms and farmers and how they came to prosper and stand on their own. My purpose is to show, by authentic experience in one American region, that to get such new jobs and factories and fertile farms our choice need not be between extremes of "right" and "left," between overcentralized Big-government and a do-nothing policy, between "private enterprise" and "socialism," between an arrogant red-tape-ridden bureaucracy and domination by a few private monopolies. I have tried in these pages to express my confidence that in tested principles of democracy we have ready at hand a philosophy and a set of working tools that, adapted to this machine age, can guide and sustain us in increasing opportunity for individual freedom and well-being.

This confidence that *it can be done,* that the fog, and the fears its shadowy shapes engender, will vanish if we look at the reality and not the words, is based on ten years of experience in the Tennessee Valley. Here the people and their institutions —among them the regional development corporation known as TVA—have provided just such a demonstration of the vitality of democracy. It is that ten years of actual experience—the background for this book—that reveals the promise and the hope of tomorrow for men everywhere.

I am an administrator and not a professional writer. This book bears the literary marks of that deficiency. I have had to do the writing, moreover, while carrying on my work, often in the midst of those recurrent "crises" that make up the life of any administrator. And I recognize that in writing about the Tennessee Valley Authority I cannot be wholly objective. No one can be so absorbed in this work as for a decade I have been and remain thus passionless about a task so altogether heartening. The reader, then, is warned at the outset that he will find no tone of Olympian neutrality in this book. For this I make no apology, for I believe the world badly needs conviction; it has had too much of a kind of impartiality that is inevitably irresponsible. In this book there are convictions stated and conclusions pressed.

This book does not purport to be a full account of the TVA. Except by way of the briefest inventory, I have not described the engineering and technical aspects of that enterprise nor the effect of the changes in the Tennessee Valley upon the lives of particular individuals, in some ways the most interesting part of the TVA story. There is little in this book on the public power issue, although that has been the center of most controversy about the TVA in the past: for this valley that issue appears to be settled.

What I have set down in this book is a statement of my faith, and the facts and reasons that support it.

I believe men may learn to work in harmony with the forces of nature, neither despoiling what God has given nor helpless to put them to use. I believe in the great potentialities for well-being of the machine and technology and science; and though they do hold a real threat of enslavement and frustration for the human spirit, I believe those dangers can be averted. I believe that through the practice of democracy the world of technology holds out the greatest opportunity in all history for the development of the individual, according to his own talents, aspirations, and willingness to carry the responsibilities of a free man. We have a choice: to use science either for evil or for good. I believe men can make themselves free. These convictions have been fortified as I have seen them take on substance and become part of the life of this valley and of its people; and it is of this that I write in this book.

The interpretation of the TVA that I have set down is essentially a personal one, for every man necessarily sees his experiences through his own eyes. But in forming the views and ideas written into this book I am deeply in debt to many men and women, and most of all to the people who live in this valley —and that includes of course the men and women of the TVA, associates and co-workers of mine. For this reason I have dedicated the book to them—builders for democracy—farmers, managers, architects, engineers, construction workers, chemists, merchants, accountants, preachers, many different kinds of people—in the spirit of the tablets we have put upon TVA's dams, upon which appear no named hierarchy of Board of Directors or engineers, but simply the legend: "Built for the People of the United States."

A number of friends, among them TVA Board and staff colleagues, have reviewed all or parts of the manuscript, and made helpful suggestions and criticisms, for which I am grateful. I am specially and deeply indebted to two associates. At every stage of the writing Gordon R. Clapp, General Manager of TVA, has contributed ideas, criticism, editorial suggestions, and the stimulus of his clear and seminal intelligence. I am likewise specially indebted to Marguerite Owen, TVA's Washington Representative, for the benefit of her rare critical judgment, for substantial editorial assistance and many productive suggestions. My special thanks are due to Marian Reames, whose skill and patience carried this book through the many stages of its writing, from my shorthand first drafts to the last typed revision.

In the writing of this book as in everything I have undertaken in the past twenty years I have relied greatly upon the perceptive judgment of my wife, to whom I am infinitely grateful.

What the TVA owes to Senator George W. Norris the country well knows; indeed without him there would be no TVA; his statesmanship and integrity are deeply engraved upon every chapter of TVA's legislative history. And in the years since TVA was created its administrators have been privileged to draw deeply from those well-springs of wisdom and sagacity that mark Senator Norris as one of the great men of America's history. I want too to record the very special debt that is owing to my colleague of the whole period covered by this account, Harcourt A. Morgan, the noblest and most comprehending man I have ever known. He is a great teacher of fundamentals —for a whole valley.

Finally, in addition to the impersonal words that appear in the text of this book, I want to add a word of appreciation to the President of the United States; not only for his unfailing support of TVA's basic principles of conservation and decentralization, for the establishment of which he was largely responsible, but even more for his years of warmhearted and friendly counsel and encouragement.

D. E. L.

Pine Road
Norris, Tennessee
October 6, 1943

T V A

Democracy on the March

Chapter 1

ONE VALLEY—AND A THOUSAND

T HIS book is being written in the valley of a great American river, the Tennessee. It is about that river, and that valley; about the soil of its farms, the white oak and pine on its mountain slopes, the ores and minerals that lie buried in its hills. It is about the rain that falls so violently upon its fields, and the course the water follows as it seeks out first the streams and then the river itself. This book is about the people of this valley region, the men who work the land, the men who roll the silver sheets of aluminum, who run the cotton gins, and stand behind the counter in the general stores. It is about the women who tend the spindles or stir the kettles or teach the children in the schools.

This is the story of a great change. It is an account of what has happened in this valley in the past ten years, since Congress set the Tennessee Valley Authority to the task of developing the resources of this region. It is a tale of a wandering and inconstant river now become a chain of broad and lovely lakes which people enjoy, and on which they can depend, in all seasons, for the movement of the barges of commerce that now nourish their business enterprises. It is a story of how waters once wasted and destructive have been controlled and now work, night and day, creating electric energy to lighten the burden of human drudgery. Here is a tale of fields grown old and barren with the years, which now are vigorous with new fertility, lying green to the sun; of forests that were hacked and despoiled, now protected and refreshed with strong young

1

trees just starting on their slow road to maturity. It is a story of the people and how they have worked to create a new valley.

I write of the Tennessee Valley, but all this could have happened in almost any of a thousand other valleys where rivers run from the hills to the sea. For the valleys of the earth have these things in common: the waters, the air, the land, the minerals, the forests. In Missouri and in Arkansas, in Brazil and in the Argentine, in China and in India there are just such rivers, rivers flowing through mountain canyons, through canebrake and palmetto, through barren wastes—rivers that in the violence of flood menace the land and the people, then sulk in idleness and drought—rivers all over the world waiting to be controlled by men—the Yangtze, the Ganges, the Ob, the Parana, the Amazon, the Nile. In a thousand valleys in America and the world over there are fields that need to be made strong and productive, land steep and rugged, land flat as a man's hand; on the slopes, forests—and in the hills, minerals—that can be made to yield a better living for people.

And in foreign but no longer distant lands, in the cities and the villages in those thousand valleys, live men of a hundred different tongues and many racial strains. As you move across the boundaries men have drawn upon their maps, you find that their laws are different, as are their courts and passport regulations, and what they use for money. Different too are the words you hear, the color of men's skin, the customs in the home and in the market. But the things the people live by are the same; the soil and the water, the rivers in their valleys, the minerals within the earth. It is upon these everywhere that men must build, in California or Morocco, the Ukraine or Tennessee. These are the things they dig for and hew and process and contrive. These are the foundation of all their hopes for relief from hunger, from cold, from drudgery, for an end to want and constant insecurity. A thousand valleys over the globe and our valley here are in this way the same: everywhere what happens to the land, the forests, and the water determines what happens to the people.

The Tennessee River had always been an idle giant and a destructive one. Today, after ten years of TVA's work, at last its boundless energy works for the people who live in this valley. This is true of but few of the thousands of rivers the world over. But it can be true of many, perhaps most. The job will be begun in our time, can be well along toward fulfillment within the life of men now living. There is almost nothing, however fantastic, that (given competent organization) a team of engineers, scientists, and administrators cannot do today. Impossible things can be done, are being done in this mid-twentieth century.

Today it is builders and technicians that we turn to: men armed not with the ax, rifle, and bowie knife, but with the Diesel engine, the bulldozer, the giant electric shovel, the retort—and most of all, with an emerging kind of skill, a modern knack of organization and execution. When these men have imagination and faith, they can move mountains; out of their skills they can create new jobs, relieve human drudgery, give new life and fruitfulness to worn-out lands, put yokes upon the streams, and transmute the minerals of the earth and the plants of the field into machines of wizardry to spin out the stuff of a way of life new to this world.

Such are the things that have happened in the Tennessee Valley in the past ten years. Here men and science and organizing skills applied to the resources of waters, land, forests, and minerals have yielded great benefits for the people. And it is just such fruits of technology and resources that people all over the world will, more and more, demand for themselves. That people believe these things can be theirs—this it is that constitutes the real revolution of our time, the dominant political fact of the generation that lies ahead. No longer do men look upon poverty as inevitable, nor think that drudgery, disease, filth, famine, floods, and physical exhaustion are visitations of the devil or punishment by a deity.

Here is the central fact with which statesmanship tomorrow must contend. The political promises that will be made and the great popular movements that will rise will deal with the demands of people for the ever larger harvest that science and nature, devoted to a common purpose, can be made to yield. The terms under which the people of the world will receive the products of technical advance, such as those that have come to this valley in the decade past, are at the vortex of the cyclonic forces of our century.

This hour, moreover, is the right time for telling of such things. In the desperation of a fight to survive, miracles have been wrought in laboratories and with machines. Seeing the reality of things they had never dreamed could happen, men have been deeply stirred; now almost nothing seems impossible. Whether on the fighting fronts or tending the home sector, men are thinking of tomorrow, thinking of it with longing tinged with fear and uncertainty, livened with hopes for the future. Those who fight and others who produce that their brothers may be able to fight want an earnest of good faith as to that future— things that they can see, can themselves experience. They seem no longer greatly moved and lifted by abstractions. Their thinking is less complicated but closer to life than that of the intellectual on the lecture platform or the political leader drafting a manifesto.

The fight itself comes first. But beyond that there are pictures in the recesses of men's thought behind the fighting: sixty acres of land, how it can be brought back to fertility; how to dehydrate or freeze the crop for the best kind of market; how to get back on a job at a new kind of factory machine at good pay; about a pleasant town where the kids can have bicycles; about electric lights and heated schools and churches and hospitals for the ill; no more flooding out every spring; long Diesel barges on the river to carry off the warehoused wheat; refrigerators and irrigation canals and an end to the malaria mosquitoes. The word spreads that these and many other such things can be realized after the war, that the inventors and engineers and chemists can make them happen. The word has spread to the crossroad towns in the Ozarks, the trailer camps in Detroit, the boarding houses in Fall River; to men in the oil fields across the Rio Grande, the collieries in Wales, the shops of Leeds and Manchester; even to the villages on the Ganges and the caves beneath Chungking.

Our faith is sustained by the inspiring words of great leadership, by the pledges of freedom and prosperity and democracy. But it is when the words unbend—when they come into men's homes, to their farms, their shops—that they come alive to men. Do the words mean that a livelihood will not always be won at the cost of such drudgery for men and women, will not always be so skimpy and bitter? What of the soil of their land—will it always be so starved? What of the metal that could be made of the minerals, and the houses of the forests; what of the gadgets to pump the water that for so long the women have carried in buckets day after day? What of the river that flows through the valley—what great things would happen if its flow could turn the wheels of new factories? This is a job of building for the new skills of young engineers and chemists and the Army-trained mechanics; a job for the architects and engineers with ideas about new kinds of cities, for the physicians with ideas for new kinds of hospitals and revolutions in nutrition.

The inspiring principles—is this what they mean? To give them such a meaning takes more than words and promises, however eloquent and honestly uttered. This is a job of work to be done, a job for which there is already some experience and more than enough talent and skill. The words of promise can be made to come true. Here is the Grand Job of This Century.

But everything depends upon *how* this job is done.

The spirit in which the task is undertaken; its purpose, whether for the welfare of the many or the few; the methods chosen—these will determine whether men will live in freedom and peace, whether their resources will be speedily exhausted or will be sustained, nourished, made solid beneath their feet not only for themselves but for the generations to come.

The physical achievements that science and technology now make possible *may bring no benefits,* may indeed be evil, unless they have a moral purpose, unless they are conceived and carried out for the benefit of the people themselves. Without such a purpose, advances in technology may be disastrous to the human spirit; the industrialization of a raw material area may bring to the average man only a new kind of slavery and the destruction of democratic institutions.

But such a moral purpose alone is not enough to insure that resource development will be a blessing and not a curse. Out of TVA experience in this valley I am persuaded that to make such a purpose effective two other principles are essential.

First, that resource development must be governed by the unity of nature herself.

Second, that the people must participate actively in that development.

The physical job is going to be done; of that I think we can be sure. But if, in the doing, the unity of nature's resources is disregarded, the price will be paid in exhausted land, butchered forests, polluted streams, and industrial ugliness. And, if the people are denied an active part in this great task, then they may be poor or they may be prosperous but they will not be free.

Is it inescapable that such a task of resource development be carried on only by highly centralized government direction? Must it inevitably be run by a privileged élite of managers or experts or politicians? Yes, say the defeatists about democracy, the cynics, the disillusioned and frustrated liberals, the believers in force, the disbelievers in men. Can it be done in no other way than by gutting the resources of nature, by making the country-side hideous, by maiming the forests, fouling the streams, ignoring the unity of land and water and men? Yes, that is "the way things are," say the greedy, the short-sighted, the unperceptive.

The experience in this valley gives the lie to such answers and to those who utter them. The whole point of the TVA experience that I shall seek to make plain in this book is that the best way, perhaps the only way the job can be done effectively is by observing the unity of nature, by following democratic methods, by the active daily participation of the people themselves.

What has gone on in the Tennessee Valley and what I shall describe in this book is specific, graphic, particular, something that can be seen, appraised, analyzed. One demonstration is worth much generalized discussion and tall talk. TVA was initiated frankly as an experiment; it has been administered in the spirit of exploration and innovation. But it is no utopian Brook Farm experiment; no endeavor to escape into a simpler past or a more romantic future. TVA and this valley face the facts of the present with all its complexities and difficulties.

The methods of democratic development represented by the TVA are distinctive, but their roots lie deep in the soil of American tradition and common experience. They are methods that differ from those customarily employed both by private enterprisers and public agencies. Nevertheless the TVA experiment has been carried on under the existing rules of the game of American life. It required no change in the Constitution of the United States. Congress has maintained full control. Property rights and social institutions have undergone no drastic amendment. In short, the valley's change has gone forward under typical and traditional American conditions, rather than under non-existent "ideal" conditions that would not or could not be duplicated.

The breadth of purpose and the distinctive methods of the TVA—these it is that constitute the most important part of the enterprise. It is these that will have the greatest usefulness to other Americans and to the increasingly large number of responsible men in other nations who are concerned with problems essentially similar to those that faced this valley ten years ago.

It is upon such purposes and methods that our answers to issues of peace and freedom will turn. All else—"principles" of economics and finance, dollars and pounds sterling, tariffs and taxation, unemployment insurance, health programs, new gadgets and plastics and chemicals and electronic devices, democratic government, even essential international arrangements—will depend upon the decisions we make and the course we follow tomorrow in the fundamental activity of developing the resources in the soil, the air, the water, and within the earth, through modern skills of science and organization.

Chapter 2

A RIVER IS PUT TO WORK FOR THE PEOPLE

THIS is an entirely different region from what it was ten years ago. You can see the change almost everywhere you go. You can see it in the copper lines strung along back country roads, in the fresh paint on the houses those electric lines were built to serve. You can see it in new electric water pumps in the farmyards, in the community refrigerators at the crossroads, in the feed grinders in the woodsheds. You can see the factories that stand today where there were worn-out cotton fields and rows of tenant shacks a few years ago. You can see new houses, by the thousands, on the edges of the towns—new houses of the men who take away as much cash from a few trips to the payroll window as they used to earn in a year.

You can see the change best of all if you have flown down the valley from time to time, as I have done so frequently during these past ten years. From five thousand feet the great change is unmistakable. There it is, stretching out before your eyes, a moving and exciting picture. You can see the undulation of neatly terraced hillsides, newly contrived to make the beating rains "walk, not run, to the nearest exit"; you can see the grey bulk of the dams, stout marks across the river now deep blue, no longer red and murky with its hoard of soil washed from the eroding land. You can see the barges with their double tows of goods to be unloaded at new river terminals. And marching toward every point on the horizon you can see the steel crisscross of electric transmission towers, a twentieth-century tower standing in a cove beside an eighteenth-century mountain cabin, a symbol and a summary of the change. These are among the things you can see as you travel through the Tennessee Valley today. And on every hand you will also see the dimensions of the job yet to be done, the problem and the promise of the valley's future.

A technical man will observe much that will interest him, for the Tennessee Valley Authority represents a substantial technical achievement, a record written over a wide area in concrete and steel, and in land revived and forests renewed. Here one can see what modern science can do in a few years to change the face of the earth and the waters. That technical story has been recorded with painstaking care and great detail and published in the many volumes of scientific reports by TVA's engineers, agronomists, town builders, chemists, biologists, foresters, public health experts, architects.

These technical reports will interest the experts. The average citizen will measure the change through reports of another kind: in the records of new private industries established in the valley, of failing enterprises revived, more money in people's hands, less tax delinquencies, increased bank deposits, a greater volume of buying at the stores—trends clearly established before the war. The citizen may read of the decade's change in records of new public library service or state parks established where none had been before, more hospitals, county health units almost doubled, less tuberculosis and malaria and other "low-income diseases." He may read of the number of miles of lines built to bring power to the farms of the area and the rapid increase in the amount of electricity used by the people—unprecedented in this country. He may reflect on the better quality of food produced and the increased yield per acre on the land, or analyze the ton-miles of traffic increase on the river. He may figure the potential value of the millions of seedlings planted in farm woodland and forest. He may see the newly created "Great Lakes of the South," the beauty of their thousands of miles of wooded shoreline unmarred, deep blue waters set among high mountains and abounding with game fish.

Such sights and such records reflect the ways in which, as this beautiful valley has changed, the lives of several million fellow Americans have also changed.

The story of the change begins with the river. On the map the river's five mountain tributaries, each a considerable stream —the French Broad, the Holston, the Hiwassee, the Little Tennessee, the Clinch—are clearly set off from the broad main stem, the Tennessee itself, a major river of great volume, fed by the heaviest rainfall in eastern America. The map shows that main stem as a deep crescent, its source and eastern tip in the Appalachian Mountains, the dip of the crescent slicing off the northern third of Alabama, the western tip arching northward through the flat red lands of western Tennessee and Kentucky. The river flows not in one general direction, but in three; it moves southward first, then its middle course is westward, and its lower reaches turn back toward the north. A river that "flows up the map," as visitors to TVA almost invariably remark, seems to be water flowing perversely uphill, making its way more than 650 miles from Knoxville in Tennessee, in sight of the virgin timber in the Great Smoky Mountains, the highest peaks in eastern North America, to Paducah in the lowlands of Kentucky where across the broad Ohio you can see the fields of Illinois.

The valley through which the river flows actually lies in seven historic states of the Old South: the western part of the seacoast states of North Carolina and Virginia; the northern parts of Georgia, Alabama, and Mississippi; the western half of Kentucky from its southern jointure with Tennessee north to the Ohio River; and almost the whole of the wide reaches of the state of Tennessee. Less exactly, the region reaches from the mountains about Asheville west to the sluggish Mississippi at Memphis, and north and south from the old steamboat whistle landings on Ohio's shores to the cotton fields of Mississippi and the flambeau of the furnaces at Birmingham—an area all told about the size of England and Scotland, with a population of about 4,500,000 persons.

This is the river system that twenty-one dams of the TVA now control and have put to work for the people. To do that job sixteen new dams, several among the largest in America, were designed and constructed. Five dams already existing have been improved and modified. One of TVA's carpenters, a veteran who worked on seven of these dams, described this to me as "one hell of a big job of work." I cannot improve on that summary. It is the largest job of engineering and construction ever carried out by any single organization in all our history.

In heat and cold, in driving rain and under the blaze of the August sun, tens of thousands of men have hewed and blasted and hauled with their teams and tractors, clearing more than 175,000 acres of land, land that the surface of the lakes now covers. They have built or relocated more than 1200 miles of highway and almost 140 miles of railroad. With thousands of tons of explosives and great electric shovels they have excavated nearly 30,000,000 cubic yards of rock and earth to prepare the foundations of these dams—an excavation large enough to bury twenty Empire State buildings. To hold the river the men of the TVA have poured and placed concrete, rock fill, and earth in a total quantity of 113 million cubic yards.

To comprehend these figures requires a few comparisons. This 113 million cubic yards of material is more than twelve times the bulk of the seven great pyramids of Egypt. Of these materials, the concrete alone poured into the TVA dams is two and a half times as much as used in all the locks and structures of the Panama Canal; is four times as much as in Boulder Dam, 1,200,000 cubic yards greater than in the Grand Coulee Dam; would build more than seven dams as large as Soviet Russia's great Dnieprostroy Dam. The Grand Coulee Dam is the largest single masonry structure yet built, and Boulder Dam the second largest. Boulder was in the process of construction for five years and took the combined efforts of six of our largest private building contractor firms. Grand Coulee took eight years to build, and ten major private construction firms were engaged on it.

Thirty-five Boulder dams or ten Grand Coulee dams could have been built with the total materials required for completion of this valley's dams, the work of a single organization. The TVA's employees in 1942 were simultaneously designing and building a dozen dams and improving four others, were erecting the South's largest steam-electric plant, and building large chemical and munitions factories, with a total of 40,000 men and women at work.

The work of the builders has made of the river a highway that is carrying huge amounts of freight over its deep watercourses. In 1942 more than 161 million ton-miles of traffic moved through locks, designed in co-operation with the Army Corps of Engineers and operated by them, which raise the barges from one lake's level to another. But in 1928 only a little more than 46 million ton-miles of traffic moved on the river; in 1933 the figure was 32 million. This was mostly sand and gravel moving in short hauls between adjacent areas, and some forest products.

Today huge modern towboats, powered by great Diesel engines, move up and down the channel, pushing double columns of barges, and the cargo is no longer limited to raw materials. Billets of steel and cotton goods come from Birmingham headed north, grain from Minneapolis, millions of gallons of gasoline, oil, machinery, merchandise, automobiles, military ambulances and jeeps. It is estimated that in 1945, when the channel will be fully completed for all the year and for the river's total length, the savings to shippers will be about three and a half million dollars each year.

Quiet cotton towns of yesterday are now busy river ports. And, as always has been true of water transportation, new industries are rising along its course. Millions of dollars have been invested and thousand of jobs created as new grain elevators, flour mills, and oil terminals have been erected along the river's banks. At Decatur in Alabama, on land where a few years ago farmers were raising corn and cotton, now newly built ocean-going vessels go down the ways into "Wheeler Lake" and thence to their North Atlantic job.

And on these same lakes are thousands of new pleasure craft of every kind—costly yachts, sailboats, homemade skiffs. Nine thousand miles of shoreline—more than the total of the seacoast line of the United States on the Atlantic, the Pacific, and the Gulf of Mexico—are available for the recreation of the people. Thousands of acres along the shore are devoted to public parks, operated by the states, by counties, cities, and by the TVA. More than fifty boat docks serve the needs of fishermen from all parts of the United States. By patient scientific methods designed to give nature a chance, the number of fish has been increased fortyfold in the storage reservoirs, fifteen times in the main stream reservoirs. More than forty species of fish have been caught in these lakes—a variety comparable to that of the Great Lakes. Here is the basis of a thriving industry that in 1943 produced six million pounds of edible fish, and is expected to increase to twenty-five million pounds a year.

Before the men of the Tennessee Valley built these dams, flooding was a yearly threat to every farm and industry, every town and village and railroad on the river's banks, a barrier to progress. Today there is security from that annual danger in the Tennessee Valley. With the erection of local protective works at a few points this region will be completely safe, even against a flood bigger than anything in recorded history. A measure of protection resulting from the Tennessee's control extends even beyond this valley; for no longer will the Tennessee send her torrents at flood crest to add what might be fatal inches to top the levees and spread desolation on the lower Ohio and the Mississippi.

In others of the earth's thousand valleys people live under the shadow of fear that each year their river will bring upon them damage to their property, suffering, and death. Here the people are safe. In the winter of 1942 torrents came raging down this valley's two chief tributaries, in Tennessee and Virginia. Before the river was controlled this would have meant a severe flood; the machinery of vital war industries down the river at Chattanooga would have stopped, under several feet of water, with over a million dollars of direct damage resulting.

But in 1942 it was different. Orders went out from the TVA

office of central control to every tributary dam. The message came flashing to the operator in the control room at Hiwassee Dam, deep in the mountains of North Carolina: "Hold back all the water of the Hiwassee River. Keep it out of the Tennessee." The operator pressed a button. Steel gates closed. The water of that tributary was held. To Cherokee Dam on the Holston went the message: "Keep back the flow of the Holston." To Chickamauga Dam just above the industrial danger spot at Chattanooga: "Release water to make room for the waters from above."

Day by day till the crisis was over the men at their control instruments at each dam in the system received their orders. The rate of water release from every tributary river was precisely controlled. The Tennessee was kept in hand. There was no destruction, no panic, no interruption of work. Most of the water, instead of wrecking the valley, actually produced a benefit in power, when later it was released through the turbines.

Back of the orders from the water dispatcher to the men who operate the dams is an elaborate system of reporting rainfall and gauging the flow of streams so the height of waters can be predicted for days in advance. To the head of the TVA forecasting division, from all over the watershed, from every tributary stream, from three hundred stations, by teletype, telephone, and shortwave radio come reports of the river's "stages," i.e., its height. Here, for example, is one of the messages that came from H. S. Barker near Mendota, in Virginia, during the critical days of the 1942 flood:

River three feet eighty-four hundredths raining rainfall one seventeen hundredths inches.

That is, river stage was 3.84 feet; it was raining at the time; the rainfall during the past twenty-four hours was 1.17 inches.

Reports come in from hundreds of remote rain-gauge stations, telephoned in by a farmer's wife, a crossroad store merchant, a woodsman. From well-nigh inaccessible mountain streams ingenious TVA-made devices send in their reports by shortwave

radio without human intervention. And all the reports are combined and interpreted by engineers, so that they know almost
exactly how much water will be swelling the river the next day
and the next. Yesterday's reports are checked with today's and
revised tomorrow, and the best technical judgment is sent to
the river control room: just how much water is being added to
the river's flow in the French Broad, the Holston, the Clinch,
the Hiwassee.

The operating orders go out, turning water off or on to meet
the demands of the crisis along a watercourse from the headwaters of the Tennessee to the Gulf, almost as long as the
Mississippi from its headwaters to New Orleans. The Tennessee River throughout its length is controlled, as water is
retained at one dam, released at another. This valley has been
made safe.

This is not true of other river valleys. Here, for example, is a
press association dispatch of May 13, 1943:

Swollen creeks and rivers flooded more than one million acres of
low-lying farmlands in six states Thursday, burying spring crops,
blocking highways and taking at least seven lives.

High water left hundreds of farm families homeless as flood crests
rolled downstream in Arkansas, Oklahoma, Kansas, Missouri, Indiana,
and Illinois. . . .

As the river crest moved downstream Army engineers retreated
before it, abandoning levee after levee as the hopelessness of combat-
ing the flood became apparent.

A few days later this summary appeared in the New York
Times (May 27, 1943):

During May muddy waters have submerged 3,926,000 acres in
Illinois, Missouri, Arkansas, Oklahoma, Kansas and Indiana, routed
160,000 persons and caused twenty-one deaths in the worst floods in
the midlands since 1937, when the Ohio and Mississippi Valley
disaster made more than 1,000,000 persons homeless and took 466
lives.

All over the world the story is much the same. Here, for example, is a newspaper account from New Delhi, India, dated August 7, 1943:

Approximately 10,000 Indians were drowned in the past week by floodwaters of the Khari River which swept suddenly through nearly 100 villages. Nearly a sixth of the tiny British Province of Ajmer-Merwara was under water.

And in the fall of 1943 came that flood's horrible sequel: famine.

No major river in the world is so fully controlled as the Tennessee, no other river works so hard for the people, for the force that used to spend itself so violently is today turning giant waterwheels. The turbines and generators in the TVA powerhouses have transformed it into electric energy. And this is the river's greatest yield.

Chapter 3

TWELVE BILLION GENII

IN TEN years the dams TVA has built have made this region the second largest producer of power in the United States. In 1944 the system will yield a total of twelve billion kilowatt hours of electric energy, nearly half as much electricity as the utilities in the entire country produced when we entered World War I.

These figures have deep human importance, for this must be remembered: the quantity of electrical energy in the hands of the people is a modern measure of the people's command over their resources and the best single measure of their productiveness, their opportunities for industrialization, their potentialities for the future. A kilowatt hour of electricity is a modern slave, working tirelessly for men. Each kilowatt hour is estimated to be the equivalent of ten hours of human energy; the valley's twelve billion kilowatt hours can be thought of as 120 billion man hours applied to the resources of a single region! This is the way by which, in the Age of Electricity, human energies are multiplied.

Ten years ago the per capita electricity production in the TVA area was about 60 per cent of the per capita average for the United States; today the figure is half again as great as the United States average. Here in the past decade the amount of electricity produced, per person, increased 500 per cent, twice as fast as in the United States as a whole. Ten years ago the estimated annual power production per person in the Tennessee Valley area, as nearly as can be computed, was only 400 kilowatt hours; in 1943 this had increased almost six times to 2,400 kilowatt hours, to be compared with the annual production per person of 1,530 kilowatt hours for the United States as a whole. (These figures result from dividing the total amount of electricity produced in a region by the population of the area in which it was used; they should not be confused with the average use of electricity per domestic customer, to which I shall refer later.)

Plans for the industrialization of undeveloped countries invariably begin with the production of electric power. This was true in Soviet Russia, where even as recently as 1935 (later figures are not available) the total electrical energy per person was only 141 kilowatt hours; in China the figure is only 5.1. A high production of electricity per person of population is a requisite of a technical society.

Where does this valley's vast amount of electricity go? Ever since the fall of France most of it has gone directly into war production. For electric power is the lifeblood of modern warfare. Take aluminum, for example. This valley's power has produced a major part of the aluminum for American aircraft—at one critical phase of the war more than half—and aluminum is mostly the product of electric power: as much electricity goes into one big bomber as the average household would consume in four hundred years.

But aluminum is only one example of the war use of power produced by TVA. Six basic materials plants, located here since 1933, before the outbreak of war in Europe, alone use as much electric power as all the people and all the industries of Pittsburgh or Boston, and up and down the valley are many smaller industrial plants, their furnaces heated, their motors turned by the controlled waters of the river. They are processing metals, food, fibers, timber products, chemicals, producing airplanes, boilers for ships, gas masks, and explosives. TVA's own chemical plants are now using power for the same military purpose: to make the ingredients of smoke screens, explosives, incendiary bombs, synthetic rubber. And that is where most of the power

of the river will continue to go until the war is won. The valley
will be ready when that day comes to turn that rush of energy
once again into the building of a region for peace.

The power of the river spreads its way all over the land of
the valley. Power has come to the farms of the region, 85,000 of
them in seven states, about one in every five. Ten years ago there
was electricity on only one Mississippi farm out of a hundred;
in Georgia one out of thirty-six; in Tennessee and Alabama one
in twenty-five. In this decade the rate of increase has been about
three times as fast as in the country as a whole. We still have a
long way to go. After the war, when copper lines and appliances
again are available, the march of farm lines through this countryside will resume. A decade hence there will not be many
Tennessee Valley farms without electricity.

In tens of thousands of farmyards and farm homes you can
see the change this power has already wrought. There are refrigerators in the kitchens. The water is carried by an electric
pump instead of by the women, young and old, with their
water pails. There are hay driers in barns, freezing lockers
in the crossroads stores. There are community food dehydrators,
small motors to grind feed, cut the wood, turn a small lathe.
Power is curing hams, processing sweet potatoes, cooling milk
in the new dairies.

The farm people themselves are running this part of the job,
through a particular kind of TVA-inspired co-operative born
in 1934 in the back of a furniture store in Corinth, a small Mississippi town. This was the unpretentious prototype of farm electricity "co-ops" that under the REA have since spread all over
the country. You have to attend the annual meeting of one of
these co-operatives—there are now forty-five of them in five
states of the Tennessee Valley—to understand the change electricity has brought. The motors and appliances tell only a part
of the story.

I have been at such meetings where throughout a whole day
as many as two thousand farmers and their wives and children
discussed the financial and operating reports made to them by

their superintendent and board of trustees, and later while we ate a barbecue lunch watched new uses of electricity demonstrated. Some of these enterprises are large: one has 7,500 members, an investment of nearly two million dollars; another 6,700 members, a capital of $1,250,000. But these membership "town meetings" are not simply business sessions. They have an emotional overtone, a spiritual meaning to people who were so long denied the benefits of modern energy and convenience which had become a commonplace to their city neighbors. The talk still turns to the hard days before "we won our fight," to the dark difficulties that had to be gone through before the crews came down the road, the poles were set, the copper lines strung, the lights went on.

And you can follow the course of change that electricity has brought in the lives of townspeople, too, in the several hundred small communities, towns, and good-sized cities in six states, where a half million homes and places of business are served with power from their river by 129 locally owned public agencies, agencies which purchase the power at wholesale from the TVA. What has gone on there has never happened before in all the history of electricity. Ten years ago the homes of this area which had electricity used it sparingly; a large percentage of the homes had none at all. The typical use was for lighting, perhaps also for an electric iron, a radio. Today the amount of use and the number of homes that have electricity have both greatly increased.

There are few regions of the world that use power so widely. Nine out of every ten wired homes in Chattanooga, for example, now have electric refrigeration, and in Knoxville three out of every four. Electric ranges are used in nearly half the homes in Nashville which have electricity. It is much the same story all up and down the valley: in scores of small communities, in cities, in rural areas. Take the record in the home use of electricity by the first dozen distributors of TVA power, the local public agencies, which, through systems they have themselves acquired, resell TVA power at the low rates agreed upon with TVA.

When they started, the average use of electricity by their customers was 17 per cent below the national average. At the end of a two-year period the use of electricity had increased 146 per cent, 77 per cent above the nation's average household use, while the country as a whole was showing an increase of only 15 per cent. This increase was not just a flash in the pan. Between 1934 and 1942, in the homes served by these twelve original TVA distributors, the increase was 196 per cent compared with 63 per cent for the nation.

Another way of showing the effect of the change is in the increase in the number of urban homes that are using electricity for the first time. In the case of these twelve original distributors there was an increase of 58 per cent in the number of homes using electricity, while the increase in the country as a whole was only 6 per cent; between 1934 and 1942 the increase in the nation was 31 per cent, whereas in these twelve communities there were 232 per cent more electricity-using households than in 1934.

The spread of the benefits of the river's power is not uniform in every community, of course, but the general result is always the same. The percentage increases in use of electricity in some of the communities are spectacular: in some instances 200 to 300 per cent, in others even greater. Of the eighty-four municipal distributors of TVA power that have been operating two years or more, all except three exceed the national average in the use of electricity in homes, which for 1942 stood at 1,022 kilowatt hours. In the homes of forty-two of these cities and towns the average use is 50 per cent greater than the national average used. In thirteen communities the average use is 100 per cent greater than the national average.

How can one account for this unprecedented change in the use of electricity in this valley? Why is the use so much greater than in other areas that have a greater income? The answer is to be found largely in a new way of thinking about electricity, best reflected in the principle of a low rate—with a resulting wide use of power. That principle of "more not less" was established in the very policies of the Act creating the TVA. Congress directed the TVA to see to it that this vast store of electric power should be widely used; the moral purpose behind the whole TVA Act, to benefit the greatest number of people, was thus written into an express mandate of law.

To effectuate the law's policy of a wide and extensive use of electricity it was necessary for TVA to break sharply with the ways of fixing electricity rates that with few exceptions had been followed in the electrical industry. The schedule of rates we announced in September of 1933 was low, extraordinarily low, judged by the then prevailing ideas. Those retail rates were based on the principle that people wanted to use electricity not in a niggardly way, but generously and for many new uses. To reach that goal of wide use, rates had to be drastically cut. This, we were convinced, would be financially sound, for people would then *use so much more electricity* that the income of the distributors would rise proportionately. What had proved to be a good business principle for Henry Ford in the pricing of his first automobiles, what was good business in the mass production field generally, would be good business in electricity supply. It would, moreover, add to the strength and the richness of living of the people of the valley.

The particular rates embodied in the TVA schedule were not to be an absolute standard of precisely what should be charged for electricity anywhere and everywhere in the country, with the implication that any company charging more than the TVA rate was therefore proved an extortionist. The country is far too diverse, conditions are far too varied, for any such oversimplification. The example this valley has supplied is a yardstick in a much more important sense. It has been demonstrated here, to the benefit both of consumers and utilities, that drastic reductions in electric rates result in hitherto undreamed-of demands for more and more electricity in homes and on farms.

The experience of the private utilities in the area adjacent to the Tennessee Valley has shown this in an interesting way. A short time after TVA announced these low rates, the neighboring private utilities of the Southeast followed suit by making large reductions in their own rates. The immediate result was a spectacular increase in the use of electricity in the homes they served. The year after the private companies adopted the principle of the TVA yardstick, though not the rates, for theirs did not decline so far, five of the six companies in the entire United States with the greatest increase in electric growth were here in the Southeast.

Following this rate reduction, these neighboring private companies immediately outdistanced the rest of the country in the sale of electric appliances. The Georgia Power Company, for example, twenty-third in size among the utilities of the country, sold more electric refrigerators the first year of its rate reduction than any other company in the country regardless of size, was first in the sale of electric water heaters, and second in the sale of electric ranges. Its neighbor company, the Tennessee Electric Power Company, thirtieth in size in the country, immediately following this rate reduction became first in the total number of electric ranges sold, second in the number of electric refrigerators, third in the number of electric water heaters. This company, with only 100,000 residential users, was actually selling more home electric appliances than companies in high-income states like New York and Illinois with many times as many customers.

The TVA's yardstick rates have been the occasion for a great deal of controversy, and thousands of pages have been written on the subject. I do not intend in this book to add further to that output. The yardstick in its correct sense has served and continues to serve a public purpose. It has led all over the country to a realistic re-examination of the financial feasibility of low rates. It has established the fact that rates by private utilities far lower than were thought possible ten years ago are profitable.

In the Tennessee Valley these yardstick rates are now in the process of declining even further because of large cash surpluses in the hands of municipal and cooperative power distributors. After the war many of them will be in a position to reduce rates to a level 25 per cent lower, on the average, than the 1933 rates. Rates not markedly higher than those announced by TVA in 1933 and vigorously denounced at that time as "impossible" are now being charged by private utilities. They are returning a profit to the private companies in a period of higher costs. And the average residential rate for the whole country, which was 5.52 cents in 1933, was 3.67 cents in 1942, a decrease of 33⅓ per cent below 1933 levels.

The average rate paid for electricity by all ultimate consumers in the country dropped only 2 per cent in the seven years from 1926 (the first year for which the statistics are reported) to 1933, the year TVA was created. In the seven years *after* the creation of TVA the average rate paid fell 23 per cent. By 1942 the average national reduction from 1933 was practically one-third.

There were other forces at work, of course. But it is certainly clear that the lesson of the yardstick rates—known and practiced in 1933 by but a few of the electric industry's progressives, men like Ferguson of the Hartford Company and Evans of the Tacoma Municipal System—has already become common knowledge.

The sharp controversy over this matter can now be left to historians and to those rugged souls who enjoy hanging on to old issues. As a reading of this book will show, the reduction in electric rates was only a part of the TVA story, and it is to the presentation of the whole scope of the events in the Tennessee Valley that this record is directed.

Chapter 4

NEW LIFE FROM THE LAND

THE river now is changed. It does its work. But it is on the land that the people live. Millions of acres of the valley's land had lost its vitality. The people had to make it strong again and fruitful if they themselves were to be strong. For here in this valley more people depend for a living upon each acre of farm land than in any other area in America. The farms are usually small, an average of seventy-five acres. Farm families are large, and the birthrate is the highest in the United States. Many people living on impoverished land—that was the picture ten years ago. If the moral purpose of resource development— the greatest benefit to human beings—was to be achieved, TVA had to see to it that the land changed as well as the river.

And the land is changing. It is a slow job. Engineering a river with large-scale modern machinery and rebuilding soil that for generations has been losing its vitality are tasks of a different tempo. But even after these few years you can see the difference everywhere. The gullies are being healed. The scars of erosion are on the mend, slowly but steadily. The many wounds yet to be healed are by their contrast eloquent evidence of what a decade's work in restoration has accomplished. The cover of dark green, the pasture and deep meadow and upstanding fields of oats and rye, the marks of fertility and productiveness are on every hand. Matting and sloping, seeding and sodding have given protection to eroded banks on scores of thousands of acres. Ditches to divert the water and little dams to check it, hundreds of thousands of them, help control the course of the

25

water on the land, hold it there till it can soak down and feed the roots of newly planted trees and grasses. A hundred and fifty million seedling trees have been planted on hundreds of thousands of acres of land from TVA nursery stock alone.

The farmers have built terraces on a million acres and more; their graceful design, following the contour, makes a new kind of landscape, one that led Jefferson, observing the effect upon the face of his own Monticello acres, to exclaim that in "point of beauty nothing can exceed" contour plowing with its "waving lines and rows winding along the face of the hills and valleys."

And on 20,000 individual farms embracing a total area of nearly 3,000,000 acres, actual farmers selected by their neighbors are carrying on a demonstration of modern farming, sponsored by TVA, built around a more scientific use by farmers of the almost magic mineral, phosphate, and the use of power and the machine. These 20,000 farm families have been willing, at considerable individual risk, to undertake a changed way of farming. Quite aside from the effect on crop production this is a human fact of great importance.

These pioneers call themselves "demonstration farmers." They have their own county organizations known generally as Farm Improvement Associations or by similar names. Much of the story of how these demonstrations function I shall tell in a later chapter. These are private farms, not public show places. But on thousands of such farms, in every county of this Tennessee Valley—about one out of ten of the total valley farms—you get a preview of what the future promises for this whole region in the years to come. You can learn what levels of food production the remaining acres of the valley will be capable of reaching. Less than a decade ago these demonstration farms were in about as severe straits as any in our land; now you can see the rich rewards that can come to those who through science and skill and learning from each other find the way to build their land and their region.

In these past ten years farming throughout the valley has increased in yield and fruitfulness, but it is on the demonstration farms that you see the best of what this land is capable of and what farmers can do, with only small help from public expenditures. The best way to get the story of the results is from the records of the seven valley State Extension Services, the state agencies that have agreed with TVA to carry out the actual program.

The state agricultural experts tell the story in terms of greater output. Production levels throughout the valley have increased within this decade: small grains increased 13 per cent, corn was maintained at the same levels but was using fewer acres, hay increased 33 per cent. But on the demonstration farms, where these new farming methods have been put to use, the rate of increase was three times greater. Under the new way of farming, the same acreage and the same manpower now produce from 30 per cent to 60 per cent more meat, eggs, milk, and dairy products.

Out of the thousands of reports in the records of the state agricultural institutions here is one from a Tennessee county, a land of "thin soil" and struggling people. In 1939 the TVA co-operative demonstration program began; in 1942 the annual report stated:

The number of milk cows increased 70%, from 43 head in January 1939 to 73 in the fall of 1942 . . . The number of beef cattle and veal calves marketed annually from the community has doubled during the last three years . . . In addition, there has been a substantial increase in poultry and hog production for home use.

In five years one community in Virginia reports food production doubled. The director of the Extension Service wrote of the demonstration farmers:

They have twice the number of beef and dairy cattle now as in 1937. They have 24 per cent more sheep, 13 per cent more chickens and 31 per cent more brood sows.

From Kentucky came this report:

The number of livestock has more than doubled since the beginning of the demonstration four years ago. More hay and im-

proved pastures are being produced at the present time. The acreage
of corn has been reduced one third, but increased fertility has given
the same yield at less cost and less labor.

In Georgia the State Extension Director reported on progress
on 103 farms:

Cotton yields have increased from 275 to almost 400 pounds *per
acre*. Corn yields have been boosted from 20 to 30 bushels per acre.
Acreage of soil-building crops *per farm* has jumped from 10 to 35.
Animal units per farm have doubled.

This is one way agricultural experts measure how the people
have changed the land. They will tell you how the grazing
season has lengthened, how the land yields a more nutritious
grass and a better grade of corn, how every acre supports more
animals, how from every crop and every head of cattle, from
every laborer on the farm, there is greater production and more
food value in each unit produced.

They may tell you of the experience in Hamilton County,
Tennessee, where a Negro farming community entered the demonstration program in August of 1940, on worn-out soil where
corn yields ran only about ten bushels to the acre. In the fall of
1942, just two years after the experiment was started, the president of the group made this report:

The Community made 8 times as much hay in the fall of 1942 as
was formerly made in a season. . . . Ten to 12 bushels of winter
cover crop seed—crimson clover, vetch, oats and rye—were planted
in the fall of 1942. . . .
The number of milk cows in the community has been increased
from 8 to 35, work stock from 9 to 18, brood sows from none to 4,
hens from 190 to over 600.

Another way to tell the story of the changed land is to cite the
cases of individual farmers among these twenty thousand farmer
pioneers. Henry Clark is one. He began farming about ten years
ago on fifty-five acres of land in the hills of Grainger County,
Tennessee, which the Extension Service records describe as in a
"badly run-down state of cultivation . . . . Some of the fields had

even been abandoned and had a thick cover of broom sedge, pine, persimmon, and sassafrass bushes. No lime, phosphate, or complete fertilizer was ever used. Not a seed of pasture or hay had ever been sown." All the equipment Clark had was "a little black mare" and a crude sled he had built.

In the fall of 1936 Clark became a demonstration farmer. With the exception of six tons of TVA phosphate, on which Clark himself paid the freight, and the intelligent counsel of the county agricultural agent and his assistant, virtually the entire change that has taken place in these fifty-five acres has come out of the skill and devotion of Henry Clark and his wife, out of their ability to take advantage of modern agricultural knowledge, electric power, and machinery.

One would not recognize these rich pastures and fields today as those same sedge-covered, eroded slopes. A farm that could barely raise ten bushels of corn to the acre is now producing fifty to sixty bushels of oats an acre. On the now carefully ter-raced farm are deep-rooted red clover, alfalfa, and a herd of fine cattle. Instead of the little black mare and her primitive sled, Henry Clark now farms with a tractor, a mowing machine, a grain drill, and other equipment, and earns added income by doing "custom" work for others with his machinery. Each week through the year the Clarks send milk and eggs to market. Every year several calves go to the butcher, several hundred bushels of tomatoes to the truck market, together with a substantial amount of tobacco, their biggest cash crop. All this is from a farm that was practically unproductive ten years ago, the kind of land referred to in certain kinds of surveys as "submarginal," fit only for public purchase and retirement. On the farm now stands a pleasant home which Clark himself has added to and modernized, and in the kitchen are an electric range, refrigerator, and washing machine. Today he is the full owner of his farm enterprise and all its equipment. The detailed records of thou-sands of such demonstrators show wide variations in results, as one would expect; but almost without exception they tell a heartening story of changed land and changed lives.

To rebuild the soil and the farm life of the Tennessee Valley a detailed scientific survey of the quality of the various kinds of soils, probably the most intensive ever undertaken, has been going on in this region since 1933. And, as a result of soil surveys taken in a great many counties of the valley and of scientific analysis by the seven state universities on TVA's behalf, farmers can go to their county agricultural agent and learn whether their soil is Fullerton cherty silt loam or Maury silt loam or Hartselle fine sandy loam, or any one of the hundreds of types, each different from the others, each calling for different handling to get the maximum yield with the least injury to the basic resources. The soil can work for the people best when the people understand it.

But the job of test-demonstration—just another word for "learning" and "teaching," of course—extends beyond the crops and meadows and pastures, the farm house and the barn. It includes the woodland on the farm. Fifty-four per cent of this valley is wooded, and of these 14,000,000 wooded acres over 40 per cent belong to farmers.

The farmer's woodland has become a part of demonstration farming. In those woods he is growing a new crop of trees, such as black walnuts of a special strain, for example, or a fine straight species of black locust, or blight-resistant Asiatic chestnuts, or oriental persimmons. From the nursery maintained by TVA, over 110,000 grafts and cuttings of ten species and many varieties of special strains have gone out for planting by farmers. One kind of tree is chosen to be grown for fence posts, another because its branches make good cotton spindles; the nuts of this one can be sold to the shelling plant near by; one species is chosen for use as wildlife food, another for its beauty or the shade it gives for the family in the farmyard, and for the fruit pods that fatten cattle and pigs. All the trees help to save the soil, to hold the water on the land. Many of them raise the farmers' income and relieve the pressure to rely for cash upon soil-costly corn and cotton.

The plentiful rainfall and long growing season in the valley push trees along at an incredible rate. From where I write I can see a slope that nine years ago was newly planted with pine seedlings; today most of those trees are eighteen to twenty-five feet tall, and the hillside is a dense green bank. In private woodland and forest, on thousands of acres of TVA reservoir land, the forests of the valley are coming back.

Farmers, singly and in associations, are actively trying to prevent the devastation of forest fires. In thirty-three counties scientific methods of timber management and harvesting are being demonstrated; counsel is being given to forest properties totaling 200,000 acres. The industry built upon the woods, which has given employment to one out of every twelve of the valley's workers, a $112,000,000 annual business, is being shored up, its once crumbling foundation greatly strengthened. The brave new trees that you see everywhere are in the pattern of the slowly changing region.

The change is not only on the land but beneath it as well. The minerals of the earth must be made to work for the people. The Tennessee Valley has a great variety of these minerals— more than fifty. Some of them have never been put to much use, because science has thus far passed them by; the green olivine ore of North Carolina's mountains is an example. The ore is one-fourth magnesium metal. The many kinds of minerals have been sought out by TVA and their extent ascertained, in some cases by extensive drilling, so that businessmen will have a reliable basis for judging whether the ores can be transformed into jobs in a new industry.

Some of these minerals were of too low a grade to attract private industry in the pioneering years of bounty when the population was sparse, the world seemed new, and waste was commonplace. Now many of them, as experimentation sponsored by TVA has shown, can be economically used. Kaolin, a kind of clay, for example, had been known in North Carolina since colonial days, but it seemed cheaper and easier to bring clays for high-grade china from abroad than to find a way in which our own deposits could be used. To develop a refining method which would make that kaolin useful for American potteries was an early project of TVA. It proved a success. The North Carolina deposits are now extensively developed for this purpose by several private concerns.

Another mineral, low grade manganese ore, formerly was little used; now a new process makes this resource available for the steel industry. A process newly developed at Muscle Shoals by TVA engineers is able to produce aluminum from white clay abundant in Tennessee and Alabama and Mississippi. In a building adjoining the aluminum-from-clay pilot plant, tests of the new magnesium-from-olivine process move forward. In several state laboratories experiments such as these are going on under the auspices of TVA. In these developments are the signs of other changes yet to come.

Facts about the region are often just as potent tools of resource development as TVA's giant earth-movers with their nine-foot-high rubber wheels, or the tilted terracing machines. There has been carried on in this region in the past decade a gathering of facts about its resources and its institutions probably not equaled for thoroughness in any other American region.

Facts about the sanitary condition of the streams, facts about the financial structure of local government units and about the forests, about recreational possibilities, about present and future transportation arteries. Facts about the kinds of land, classified in many ways for many different purposes. Aerial photographs of every foot of the valley, maps of such detail and accuracy that TVA's mappers have been called upon by the Army to make similarly exact maps of many strategic war areas outside this region. Facts about factory buildings not now in use, which might be converted by an enterprising businessman or a war agency. Facts about how much soil was washed from a field planted in cotton, compared with that from one in pasture or in forest. Facts about the schools, hospitals, farm tenantry, about rainfall, tuberculosis, and syphilis. Facts about men and skills available for industry. Facts about industrial and domestic water supply, freight rates.

Not facts for their own sake, to be encased in dull "reports." Live facts that live people use today or will need tomorrow to help them make their decisions about industrial location, farm- ing, education, public health. The power of knowledge is also at work changing a valley, releasing the resources of the region to raise the income level of the people.

Chapter 5

THE PEOPLE'S DIVIDEND

THE story thus far as I have recounted it has been chiefly one of physical changes in the Tennessee Valley. But what has been the yield to the people—to those who live in the region, and to the people of the country as a whole who advanced most of the funds?

First of all, the level of income of the region's people is definitely rising. By 1940, and before the effect of war expansion, the per capita income had increased in the seven valley states 73 per cent over the level of 1933; while for the same period the increase in the country as a whole was only 56 per cent. The same trend is reflected in income payment statistics. Between 1933 and 1943 the seven valley states show an increase in per capita income payments which substantially exceeds the index for the country as a whole. The rate of increase in each of the seven valley states is above the index for the country. The same is true of total income payments: the rate of increase for all the valley states, and for each of the states, exceeds the national index of rate of increase. Bank deposits increased 76 per cent between 1933 and 1939 compared to 49 per cent in the country, and retail sales increased 81 per cent compared to 71 per cent for the country.

All the available figures—and the evidence of one's eyes—show that our income level is rising. But the Tennessee Valley is still a region of low income, about half the United States average.

What has happened to the businesses of the people? Farming

is the most important private enterprise in this region; that business, as I have indicated, is moving upward as the fruitfulness and stability of the land increase. What of business in the industrial sense? That too is developing, and at a rapid rate. Even before the war the valley saw the addition or expansion of several large industries devoted to the basic materials of modern industry, such as aluminum, ferro-silicon, heavy chemicals; these included two of the largest phosphatic chemical works in the country.

The war has added mightily to the list. For reasons of security little of this expansion can now be told. But when the full story of a once industrially laggard valley's part in production for war can be revealed, it will rank as one of the miracles of American enterprise, the kind of miracle that is marvelled at when it occurs across the seas, rarely comprehended close at home.

At least as important as these heavy industries is the rise of new light industries and the expansion of plants that existed before 1933. The industries added since 1933 range from those for the processing of frozen foods and the production of cheese to the manufacture of aircraft and mattresses, bottle washers, stoves, flour, inlaid wood, barrel heads and staves, electric water heaters, furniture, hats and shoes, pencils, carbon electrodes, boats, horse collars, ground mica, oxygen and acetylene, metal dies, ax handles, and barites. Many new small industries are the immediate result of opportunities for profit provided by the chain of lakes that make the Tennessee River a new arc of beauty through the countryside.

We have a long way yet to go in the valley. There are many factories yet to be built, in an area with such great potential wealth and with less than its economic share of the nation's industry and manufacturing. There are many new jobs to be created by the laboratories and businessmen out of the region's dormant resources. There are millions of acres yet to be restored to full productiveness. When TVA began its work in 1933, of the total of eight and a half million acres of cultivated land in the valley, erosion in varying degrees had damaged seven million acres. On more than a million acres the top soil had entirely disappeared. There are more trees to plant, houses, schools, roads, and hospitals to build. Many new skills have been learned —among farmers, industrial workers in the new factories, the tens of thousands of men and women who have added to their skills in the course of their work for the TVA—but lack of training is still a heavy handicap to be overcome. The task is barely begun—but the Tennessee Valley is on its way.

Democracy is on the march in this valley. Not only because of the physical changes or the figures of increased income and economic activity. My faith in this as a region with a great future is built most of all upon what I have come to know of the great capacities and the spirit of the people. The notion that has been expressed that the region's problem, as one commentator has put it, is one of "human salvage" completely misses the mark. The human resources of this valley are its greatest asset and advantage. The people have seized upon these modern tools of opportunity and have raised up their own leadership. They have shown an ability to hold themselves to tough assignments with a singleness of purpose and a resourcefulness in doing much with little that will be difficult to match anywhere in the country.

This advent of opportunity has brought with it the rise of a confident, sure, chesty feeling. The evidence is everywhere. It is epitomized in an editorial in the Decatur, Alabama, *Daily* for May 18, 1943. The editor, a community leader, candidly relates the doleful past and contrasts it with the optimistic and fruitful present. Seven years ago Decatur was in great trouble; today it is one of the most enterprising and promising small cities in the interior United States. "What has happened in these seven years?" he asks, and then he answers:

We can write of great dams . . . of the building of home-grown industry and of electricity at last coming to the farms of thousands of farm people in the Valley. *Yet the significant advance has been made in the thinking of a people.* They are no longer afraid. *They have caught the vision of their own powers.* They can stand now and talk out in meeting and say that if industry doesn't come into the Valley from other sections, then we'll build our own industry. This they are doing today.

These changes of a decade were not, of course, wrought by TVA alone: in point of fact, the very essence of TVA's method in the undertaking, as I shall later indicate in detail, was at every hand to minimize what it was to do directly and to encourage and stimulate the broadest possible *coalition* of all forces. Private funds and private efforts, on farms and in factories; state funds and state activities; local communities, clubs, schools, associations, co-operatives—all have had major roles. Moreover, scores of federal agencies co-operated—the Civilian Conservation Corps; the Department of Agriculture through such agencies as the Farm Security Administration, the Rural Electrification Administration, the scientific research bureaus, the Agricultural Adjustment Administration, the Commodity Credit Corporation, the co-operative loan banks and the Forest Service; the Public Health Service; the Army Corps of Engineers which prior to 1933 had prepared a preliminary survey of the Tennessee River widely known as "House Document 328"; the Coast Guard; the Public Works Administration; several of the bureaus of the Interior Department, the Bureau of Reclamation which prepared designs for early Norris and Wheeler dams, the Geological Survey, the Bureau of Mines, the Bureau of Fish and Wildlife Service, the National Park Service; the Geodetic Survey and the Weather Bureau—and so on; the list, if complete, would include most national agencies.

How much of the public's money has the TVA spent in these ten years? Has it been worth that cost as measured in dividends to the people?

It is as important that a public enterprise should produce

benefits and values as great as or greater than their cost as it is when the undertaking is a private one. And, to those who are studying the feasibility of developments of a comparable character, the question of cost and the balancing of investment of materials and manpower against the yield the investment produces are considerations of the first consequence.

I shall not, of course, go into all the possible technical refinements of TVA's financial affairs, since they are of little interest to the general reader. The facts are all readily available in TVA's financial statements, in its annual reports to Congress, in thousands of pages of testimony before Congressional committees, and in technical books and writings on the subject. I shall here only summarize the basic facts and the considerations that may be useful in judging the significance of those facts.

The funds used by the TVA have all been advanced from funds appropriated by Congress with two major exceptions: 65 millions of TVA bonds and about 50 millions supplied by electric rate-payers and re-invested in dams and equipment. To avoid unduly complicating the statement, however, I shall treat the funds expended as if they *all* had been advanced directly from the federal treasury; the exceptions do not affect the principles. The American people who advanced these funds are entitled to a return from them.

In judging whether they have received such a return and whether the product of TVA's investment of the people's money has been worth the outlay, it must be remembered that much of the return, to the Tennessee Valley and the nation, is in benefits which cannot be exactly measured. It is only the investment in power facilities that yields the federal taxpayers a return in dollars in addition to other benefits. For power is the only major product of the TVA investment that is sold for dollars. For the other expenditures little if any of the return is in dollars, but instead is realized in benefits to citizens and their communities and business enterprises.

The benefits of a navigable channel, for example, go to shippers, to industries using the channel, to consumers of grain, oil, gasoline, and so on. This is true, of course, not only on the Tennessee but also on the Ohio, the Illinois, the Missouri, all of the many rivers where millions of federal funds have been expended for a century and more. So it is not possible to record the same precise dollar measure of navigation benefits as it is with power. But simply because they do not appear on TVA's books as income does not mean, of course, that there are no benefits.

Likewise, the benefits of flood control produced by these dams extend all the way down the Mississippi River to the mouth of the Red. But since TVA is not paid for those benefits in dollars, the taxpayers' return cannot be measured in that way. And so it is with TVA's expenditures to produce phosphate plant food, and to demonstrate its use to control soil erosion not only in the Tennessee Valley but in Minnesota, Wisconsin, New York, Iowa, and seventeen other states outside this region. So with forestry, industrial research, mapping.

The *cost* of such development work appears on *TVA's books as a net expense*; *but the benefits appear on the balance sheet of the region and of the nation.* And, as with public improvement expenditures generally the country over, it was anticipated that such expenditures would be repaid to the taxpayers not directly in dollars, but indirectly in benefits.

Turning now to TVA's expenditures, and first the cost of developing the river: TVA's financial balance sheet shows that to provide a 650-mile navigable channel, flood protection, and power supply, the TVA has an investment in completed plant as of June 30, 1943, totaling about $475,000,000. By the end of 1944, when several dams now (September, 1943) under construction will be completed and in use, the figure will be in the neighborhood of $700,000,000. Of this amount approximately 65 per cent, or $450,000,000, will represent the power investment. The river control works will then be substantially completed.

What dividends for the people does this investment yield? Do the expenditures yield a product that justifies this cost? As to power the answer is a relatively easy one, since the power is sold and the revenues provide a dollar measurement, and one that is reassuring. In the fiscal year ended June 30, 1943, the sale of power yielded revenues to TVA in excess of $31,-500,000. Operating expenses to produce that power, including about $2,000,000 of tax payments and about $6,000,000 (or almost 20 per cent of each dollar of revenue) in depreciation charges, left a surplus of revenue over cost of more than $13,000,000.

Actual earnings in the first months of the current fiscal year indicate that the total net income from power since the beginning of the TVA in 1933 to June 30, 1944, will be well over $40,000,000. This substantial surplus will have been accumulated in only five or six years, for between 1933 and 1937 the TVA was not a going power concern; the system was incomplete and operations were beset by a multiplicity of lawsuits and injunctions which prevented the normal sale of the power produced by the river. The size of this net income indicates pretty clearly that the power asset of the Tennessee River certainly is worth its cost.

These calculations take into account only dollar returns to TVA, and none of the indirect benefits. But such benefits are many. Among them are the $10,000,000 annual savings to consumers as a result of greatly reduced rates, the effects on the region's business enterprises of large amounts of low-cost power, the benefits that have resulted to business in other regions of the country, as well as the fact that 80 per cent of the equipment and materials purchased by TVA were produced in factories located in regions outside the Tennessee Valley. Nor do they seek to measure the value to the country of the fact that it was largely because of power from this river that in 1943 America was able to build huge fleets of bombers to send over Europe and the South Pacific.

Will the current revenues and surpluses continue in the future? The end of the war will mean that large amounts of power will no longer be used for direct war production. The future of electricity, however, as an industrial necessity in the production of light metals and chemical products seems assured. The conversion of most of TVA's present industrial consumers of power to civilian production in these electro-chemical and metallurgic fields appears a reasonable prospect. There is every reason to expect a large increase in the valley's domestic and farm use of electricity, carrying forward the trend interrupted by the war. Short of a prolonged major depression after the war, power revenue will continue to cover all costs, including straight-line depreciation, and in addition will provide a large net income, probably between $10,000,000 and $15,000,000 annually.

Revenues from power and surpluses show a favorable relation to the capital invested to produce that income. On the basis of actual experience to date, power surplus could repay the American people their total power investment in TVA without interest within the next thirty years. Since much of the investment is in land or in property of almost indefinite life—a concrete dam is almost as indestructible as the rock on which it rests—this is a brief period indeed for the repayment of this investment.

At the end of that thirty-year period of repayment the situation would be this: (1) Payments from users of TVA power would have repaid to the people of the nation their total investment which has been used to transform the energy of the river into usable electricity and to construct a transmission network to reach the communities throughout the valley. (2) This $450,-000,000 property, entirely repaid by the valley consumers of TVA electricity, will be in first-class operating condition and reserves will be available to keep it intact by reason of a conservative straight-line depreciation accumulation, charged currently against the rate-payers. (3) Large surplus income from a "paid-out" investment will continue to flow into the federal treasury.

There is another way by which the soundness of the nation's power investment in the Tennessee Valley can be tested. Only a small portion of the investment, $65,000,000, is represented by bonds issued by TVA. With this exception, Congress preferred the policy of appropriating funds directly. But Congress might have followed another method. Since the federal taxpayer seems to me clearly entitled to a money return on his investment in a direct revenue-producing operation (as distinguished from an activity such as navigation or soil erosion control that does not yield revenue in dollars), Congress might have authorized TVA to issue bonds for the total power investment, with an obligation to pay interest to the private purchasers of those bonds. In this way the federal government would have shifted the burden of capital advance from general taxpayers to individual investors. The interest payments would go to those individual private investors.

If such bonds had been issued, bearing a 2 per cent interest rate, TVA surplus revenues could meet the interest payments, the physical property could be kept intact through maintenance and replacement, the investment in the property could be kept intact through straight-line depreciation charges, and sixty years from now the bonds would be completely liquidated out of earnings. If the interest rate were $2\frac{1}{2}$ per cent the same result could be reached; the retirement of the bonds would extend over a longer period, about eighty years.

These figures should be read in the light of the fact that rarely, if ever, do public utilities and railroads provide in this way for the retirement of their entire capitalization. And it is important also to bear in mind that few utilities, in whose bonds private individuals invest, follow as conservative a practice of charging depreciation as do the TVA and its associated local distributing agencies.

To sum up, in the case of the TVA (1) this method of financing would liquidate the original capital debt, (2) it would pay interest, and (3) the nation's taxpayers would still own and possess through the federal government a going concern with property intact and productive of further net income.

Inasmuch as the nation's taxpayers, though the capital they advanced will have been repaid, will still own the properties, repayment with interest in so short a period compared with the life of the properties may not be fair to this region. It may prove to be wiser to spread repayment over a longer period, and to use that added margin for reductions in TVA wholesale power rates at some future time.

By either of these measures—repayment in thirty years, or repayment in sixty or eighty years plus interest—the power investment stands as a sound proposition. But there is an additional value that attaches to the power facilities of the river not to be overlooked in resource development. For the total investment of $700,000,000 in river development produces not only power, but also the benefits of navigation and flood control. *By combining these three functions in single structures* that serve all three purposes, so that costs common to all three may be shared, great economies were produced. Navigation and flood control benefits have thereby been secured at a lower cost. Similarly, because navigation and flood control are combined in the same structure with power, power is produced more cheaply than if the sole purpose of the structure were power.

Congress directed that TVA set down on its books what appeared to the Board to be the proper portions of the total investment attributable severally to power, to navigation, and to flood control. Of the total river development investment, approximately 65 per cent will be allocated to power, 15 per cent to navigation, and 20 per cent to flood control. (These figures are tentative because not all the projects are completed as of the date of this writing.) These allocations have been made on the basis of elaborate technical studies.

Even if the total investment for power, navigation, and flood control—the entire $700,000,000—were *all* charged against power, revenues from electricity would repay that entire amount, in less than sixty years. This would be grossly unfair to electric consumers in this valley, for Congress has never applied such a policy in the development of other rivers; nor is it a policy that should be followed. I cite the fact merely to show that, regardless of how the capital cost may be allocated, this is a good investment.

The expense of providing navigation and flood control in the fiscal year 1943 was $2,035,000. This figure includes not only the costs of operation but also substantial charges for depreciation. From the beginning of the enterprise to the end of fiscal year 1943 the total net cost of supplying navigation and flood control has been about $10,000,000.

What this expenditure has yielded I have summarized in a preceding chapter. The benefits produced by these expenditures cannot be measured exactly in terms of dollars, of course. A saving of about three and a half million dollars a year already accrues to shippers using the channel; after a reasonable period of development this is expected to reach a total of more than eight million dollars annually. Savings in flood damage in a single year exceed a million dollars. The direct stimulus that this channel and flood protection have provided to the growth of private business has already been shown to be great. While it cannot be proved statistically, there is every reason to believe that the value of the benefits justifies the investment allocable to navigation and flood control, which will be about $250,000,000 and an annual operating cost, including depreciation, of about $3,000,000.

Leaving the river and turning to the cost of land restoration, TVA's balance sheet shows that in the fiscal year ended June 30, 1943, this program resulted in a net cost of $3,344,000. This includes not only the production of fertilizer but the administration of the demonstration farm activity in the Tennessee Valley and in twenty-one other states of the Union. The expense of mapping, forestry, industrial, and all other kinds of research—in short, the entire development program that I have heretofore summarized—totaled $2,595,000 for the year. These, too, are expenditures that do not yield a return in dollars, but they do yield a return in the building of a region and a nation. During the ten-year period the net expense of TVA's land restoration and all other development work has been $39,800,000; in addition $8,383,000 has been spent on fertilizer plants and equipment, including the phosphate plant at Muscle Shoals and the phosphate ore reserves, which are, of course, capital investments. The total TVA capital expenditures for every purpose whatever to June 30, 1944 (this is written in September, 1943), will be in the neighborhood of $750,000,000.

Are the expenditures for this development worth their cost to the country? There is, of course, no way of settling the question by statistical proof. You must look at the valley, appraise what the expenditure of these funds has done in increasing the productivity of the region and of the nation. You must look at the effect of the growing strength and new vitality of the valley on the total strength of the whole country in war and peace. One has to consider what it is worth to the country to provide opportunity to thousands of men and women in this valley—farmers, businessmen engaged in new enterprises, workers in new factories.

This is not a question that accountants or financial experts can answer for us. Whether the over-all results in this region are worth what they have cost is something the citizen must answer for himself as a matter not of arithmetic but of the highest public policy.

Chapter 6

A NEW WAY—AN OLD TASK

In order to master Nature we must first obey her.
— FRANCIS BACON

A NEW chapter in American public policy was written when Congress in May of 1933 passed the law creating the TVA. For the first time since the trees fell before the settlers' ax, America set out to command nature not by defying her, as in that wasteful past, but by understanding and acting upon her first law—the oneness of men and natural resources, the unity that binds together land, streams, forests, minerals, farming, industry, mankind.

This, of course, is not what the creation of TVA meant to most people who read in their newspapers of the action of Congress. For TVA was then ordinarily thought of simply as a "power" project, a venture in public ownership of hydro-electricity. And even today, in spite of its wide range of activities, it is as a "power" project that many people still regard the TVA. Why there has been this limited picture of the scope and purpose of the Authority is wholly understandable.

For fifteen years before TVA came into being Congressional and public debate centered largely on a single potential resource of the Tennessee River, hydro-electric power. For long years there had been determined efforts to dispose of the government dam and power plant at Muscle Shoals in Alabama, built with public funds for World War I, as if it were like any other of the flotsam left over from that war—the trucks and shoes and trench shovels—to be knocked down to the highest bidder. It was simply regarded as a power plant, either to be dealt with as such a plant in the hands of a private operator would be, or, if continued under public control, to be limited to the sale of generated power for distribution at a profit by private industry.

How those power facilities were to be used, that was the major question which attracted public discussion down the years. That question was settled by the passage of the Act creating TVA. But it was not settled on the narrow issue of "public ownership" of power. The message of President Roosevelt urging approval of the Norris bill (which became a law with his signature on May 18, 1933) boldly proposed a new and fundamental change in the development of our country's resources. The words of the President's message were not only eloquent; there was in them a creativeness and an insight born of his New York State experience in establishing regional planning as a political reality. That understanding was matured at his Georgia home, in long days of thinking of the problems of the South and its relation to the whole nation.

It is clear [the message read] that the Muscle Shoals development is but a small part of the potential public usefulness of the entire Tennessee River. Such use, if envisioned in its entirety, transcends mere power development: it enters the wide fields of flood control, soil erosion, afforestation, elimination from agricultural use of marginal lands, and distribution and diversification of industry. In short, this power development of war days leads logically to national planning for a complete river watershed involving many states and the future lives and welfare of millions. It touches and gives life to all forms of human concerns.

The President then suggested

legislation to create a Tennessee Valley Authority—a corporation clothed with the power of government but possessed of the flexibility and initiative of a private enterprise. It should be charged with the broadest duty of planning for the proper use, conservation, and development of the natural resources of the Tennessee River drainage basin and its adjoining territory for the general social and economic welfare of the Nation. This authority should also be clothed with the necessary power to carry these plans into effect. Its duty should be the rehabilitation of the Muscle Shoals development and the co-ordination of it with the wider plan.

Many hard lessons have taught us the human waste that results from lack of planning. Here and there a few wise cities and counties have looked ahead and planned. But our Nation has "just grown." It is time to extend planning to a wider field, in this instance comprehending in one great project many States directly concerned with the basin of one of our greatest rivers.

The TVA Act was nothing inadvertent or impromptu. It was rather the deliberate and well-considered creation of a new national policy. For the first time in the history of the nation, the resources of a river were not only to be "envisioned in their entirety"; they were to be developed *in that unity with which nature herself regards her resources*—the waters, the land, and the forests together, a "seamless web"—just as Maitland saw "the unity of all history," of which one strand cannot be touched without affecting every other strand for good or ill.

Under this new policy, the opportunity of creating wealth for the people from the resources of this valley was to be faced as a single problem. To integrate the many parts of that problem into a unified whole was to be the responsibility of one agency. The Tennessee Valley's resources were not to be dissected into separate bits that would fit into the jurisdictional pigeon-holes into which the instrumentalities of government had by custom become divided. It was not conceded that at the hour of Creation the Lord had divided and classified natural resources to conform to the organization chart of the federal government. The particular and limited concerns of private individuals or agencies in the development of this or that resource were disregarded and rejected in favor of the principle of unity. What God had made one, man was to develop as one.

"Envisioned in its entirety" this river, like every river in the world, had many potential assets. It could yield hydro-electric power for the comfort of the people in their homes, could promote prosperity on their farms and foster the development of industry. But the same river by the very same dams, if they were wisely designed, could be made to provide a channel for navigation. The river could also be made to provide fun for fishermen and fish for food, pleasure from boating and swimming, a water supply for homes and factories. But the river also presented an account of liabilities. It threatened the welfare of the people by its recurrent floods; pollution from industrial wastes and public sewage diminished its value as a source of water supply and for recreation; its current carried to the sea the soil of the hills and fields to be lost there to men forever.

To a single agency, the TVA, these potentialities of the river for good and evil were entrusted. But the river was to be seen as part of the larger pattern of the region, one asset of the many that in nature are interwoven: the land, the minerals, the waters, the forests—and all of these as one—in their relation to the lives of the valley's people. It was the total benefit to all that was to be the common goal and the new agency's responsibility.

That is not the way public resource development had heretofore been undertaken in this country. Congress in creating TVA broke with the past. No single agency had in this way ever been assigned the unitary task of developing a river so as to release the total benefit from its waters for the people. Not far from where I write are other rivers developed by private interests or public agencies. They will serve to illustrate the contrast. On these rivers it is the common practice in public projects as well as private to build a single dam without first having fixed upon a general plan that will ultimately insure the full use of the whole river as a unit. There are dams built for the single purpose of power development. Such individual dams, in order to yield an immediate return in power, impair or destroy the river's full development of power at other sites, for they were not designed or built with the whole river thought of as it is in nature, a unit. These power dams are not built or operated to control floods, and do not provide a continuous navigable channel. The full usefulness of that river is lessened. Similarly, hundreds of millions of dollars in public funds have been expended for the single purpose of navigation on some of our rivers, but most of the dams constructed will not control the rivers' floods or create electric energy. They now stand as massive barriers against the erection of multi-purpose structures.

Over a long period of years scores of millions of dollars have been spent for levees to hold the waters back on the lower reaches of some of our rivers, but at the headwaters there were no reservoir dams that could make local levee protection effective.

And through the long years there has been a continuing disregard of nature's truth: that in any valley of the world what happens on the *river* is largely determined by what happens on the *land*—by the kind of crops that farmers plant and harvest, by the type of machines they use, by the number of trees they cut down. The full benefits of stream and of soil cannot be realized by the people if the water and the land are not developed in harmony.

If the soil is exposed, unprotected from the rains by cover and by roots, the people will be poor and the river will be muddy, heavy with the best soil of the fields. And as a consequence each year the farmers will be forced more and more to use their land in ways that speed up this cycle of ruin, until the cover and then the top soil itself are wholly gone. When that day comes, as in the great reaches of China's sorrowful Yellow River Valley, then the rains run off the land almost as rapidly as water runs from a pavement. Even a moderate rainfall forces the river from its banks, and every downpour brings disastrous floods, destroying crops and homes and bridges and highways, not only where the land is poor, but down the river's length, down in the areas where people are more prosperous, where the soil is still protected and factories have been built at the river's bend. Industries and railroads will be interrupted, farms flooded out, towns and villages destroyed, while heavy silt deposits fill the power reservoirs and stop up the channels of navigation.

It is otherwise where land is covered with sod or trees, and cultivated each season with the purpose of holding the rain where it falls. Such land literally serves as a water reservoir, a part of a system of flood control and river development, quite as directly as dams that stretch from bank to bank to hold the waters back. In many locations, after such proper land-use programs have been rather fully developed, the results should make it possible to reduce the magnitude and cost of engineering structures required for water control.

The farmers' new pastures and meadows themselves are reservoirs. If the changed farming practices now in use on many tens of thousands of Tennessee Valley farms were applied to all the agricultural area of our watershed (as some day I am confident they will be), the soil might absorb as much as half the customary twelve-inch surface run-off of rain each year; this storage of water on the farms would equal the capacity of two reservoirs as great as the one behind the Norris Dam, which stands 267 feet above the Clinch River.

This is of course nothing new, nothing discovered by the TVA. That a river could offer many benefits and a variety of hazards, that its improvement through engineering structures is inseparable from the development and use of the land of the watershed, has been recognized for many years by scientists and engineers. For over a generation a distinguished line of conservationists had seen this truth and written and spoken of it with great force. And as a matter of fact almost any farmer, standing in his barn door while he watches a torrential rain beat upon his land and fill his creek, could see that much. The point is that knowledge of this inseparability of land and streams has only once, here on this river, been carried into our national *action*. On every other watershed we turn our rivers over to engineers of one agency to develop while farm experts of other agencies concern themselves with the land. Thus far it is only in the Valley of the Tennessee that Congress has directed that these resources be dealt with as a whole, not separately.

The principles of unity whereby this valley has gone about the restoration of its land and the multiplication of the land's usefulness are, of course, the same as those that governed turning the river to man's account. The development of soil and its increased productivity are not simply problems of land, of farming, and of agricultural science, any more than the development of a river is only water control, dams, and engineering techniques. The restoration of land fertility, the healing of gullies, the reforestation of hillsides, these are no more ends in themselves than are flood control, navigation, and power. As the river is not separable from the land, so the land is inseparable from the forests and minerals, from the factories and shops, from the people making their living from their resources.

Here, too, the methods this valley has followed to achieve its purposes break sharply with those long prevailing. The methods differ because to think of resources as a unity compels the use of different ways. The idea of unity makes it inescapable that each man's farm must also be seen as one operating unit. The farm, too, is a "seamless web."

To the farmer on his land the problems do not fit into neat cubicles labeled "forestry" or "soil chemistry" or "mechanical engineering," nor to him is soil erosion or holding water on the land separate from the whole business of making a living on the land. And so in the way TVA goes about its responsibilities there are no "jurisdictional" lines, no excluding of the chemical engineer, say, because this is a "farm" problem, or of the businessman or the inventor because soil erosion is a "public issue," or of a county or state expert because agriculture is a "national" question. The invention by this valley's technicians of a new kind of machine and the decision of a businessman to produce and market it may be as important in land restoration as check dams in the gullies, if it thereby enables the farmer to make a living by raising soil-conserving crops. The invention here of a quick-freezing machine, a portable thresher, or a furrow seeder, all designed to overcome specific economic obstacles in the farmer's path toward land conservation, we see as just as real factors in land restoration as the terracing of the slopes.

Because they sinned against the unity of nature, because they developed some one resource without regard to its relation to every other resource in the life of man, ancient civilizations have fallen into decay and lie buried in oblivion. Everywhere in the world the trail of unbalanced resource development is marked by poverty, where prosperity seemed assured; by ugliness and desolation, with towns now dying that once were thriving; by land that once supported gracious living now eroded and bare, and over wide areas the chill of death to the ambitions of the enterprising young and to the security of the mature.

How industry came to Ducktown in the mountains of eastern Tennessee a generation ago is one such story. Copper ore was discovered; mining began; a smeltery was built. One of the resources of this remote region was being developed; it meant new jobs, income to supplement farming and forestry. But the developers had only copper in their plans. The magnificent hardwood forests to a distance of seven miles were cut and burned as fuel for the smelter's roasting ovens. The sulphur fumes from the stacks destroyed the thin cover that remained; not only the trees but every sign of living vegetation was killed and the soil became poison to life.

The dead land, shorn of its cover of grass and trees was torn mercilessly by the rains; and the once lovely and fruitful earth was cut into deep gullies that widened into desolate canyons twenty and more feet deep. No one can look upon this horror as it is today without a shudder. Silt, swept from unprotected slopes, filled the streams and destroyed fish life. The water was robbed of its value for men, for animals, and for industry, while farther down the stream a reservoir of a private power company was filling with silt. One of Ducktown's resources, copper, had been developed. But all its other resources had been destroyed in the process. The people and their institutions suffered in the end.

All this desolation caused as much pain to the officials of the copper company as it did to the lovers of nature. For balanced resource development is not, as the naïve appear to believe, a simple moral tale of "bad men" versus "good men." It is much more than that. It is the reflection of our national thinking. In fact, in this case, the early operators came to see the point better than most people, for they had to pay cash in damages for some of this destruction, after long and bitter lawsuits by the injured landowners.

The fumes from Ducktown's copper smelteries are harmless now. Indeed, in the hands of a successor company a new technical process that makes the fumes harmless yields a by-product —sulphuric acid—now more valuable than the copper itself. The copper company itself is co-operating actively with the TVA in an extensive, though still experimental, reforestation program on the area the fumes destroyed. What it has already cost and what it ultimately will cost, in manpower, materials, and the dollars of taxpayers, because copper was developed rather than the resources of Ducktown as a unity, has never been calculated. But the bill will be high.

This case seems to be extreme only because the accounting came quickly and was so clearly evident to the eye. It often takes some time before the balance shows that more is being subtracted than added from the assets of a region. But there is no escape from the arithmetic. The fall in the "water table," the sub-surface level of water, threatens industry's water supply in the Ohio Valley. The forest areas of northern Wisconsin and Michigan are dotted with towns that are dying and people who are stranded and poor. Lumber was "developed" from the wealth of the forests; there was prosperity for a time. But farming and fish and game were destroyed, and eventually the forests. Now in some regions there is next to nothing to support the towns, the highways and the schools and human beings. Unless the benefit of the people is the purpose, and the principle of the unified development of resources is the method, the harvest in the end is only such bitter fruits as these.

The "played-out" farmlands of the South, now in the process of rebuilding, were "mined" to grow a single crop of cotton: they are one more illustration of the remorseless arithmetic of nature. Here once lovely manor houses stand seedy and deserted because their foundation, the soil, has been exhausted, romantic monuments to a national tragedy of waste. And the great towers of Manhattan and Chicago, the modern business streets of Omaha on the prairies, all rest on the same foundations as the old plantation manor—the land, the waters, the minerals, and the forests. We are all in this together, cities and countryside.

There is no security or safety for us anywhere if nature's resources are exhausted. This day of machines and increasing populations multiplies our jeopardy. For this we must remember: Unless nature's laws of restoration are observed, modern technology can compress a once gradual process of resource exhaustion into the quick cycle of a generation or two.

The effect of large supplies of low-cost electricity upon industrialization illustrates the modern hazard. For electricity is not freed of these dangers simply because it is publicly owned, as some single-track enthusiasts would appear to imply. Electric power from the Tennessee River has had a great deal to do with the very considerable expansion of industry in this valley in the past decade. Indeed, it is a *sine qua non* of heavy industry, whether in India, in China, in Arkansas, or in the Balkans. It was with electricity that the transformation of rural Russia into an industrial and military giant began. It can bring great benefit to the people. But it may bring disaster. For the stimulation of industrial development by large supplies of electricity, unless the principles of unity govern, can hasten the destruction of natural resources and bring closer the day of decline.

Electric power, like the products of other resources, can be used as part of a balanced and unified program of development, and thereby further the permanent well-being of the people. Electricity is the most humane and the most efficient form of energy. It is mobility itself: It can be brought to people; people need not be brought to the source of energy. Electricity symbolizes the multiplication of human energies through science. But benefit, lasting and secure, will result only if the potentialities of power are seen as a whole, utilized not as ends in themselves but to aid in sustaining and restoring resources; this book will contain many illustrations of that kind of development in the wake of power that serves the conservation of resources.

For when a people or a region rely almost exclusively for their living upon the extraction of raw materials—the cutting of lumber, the growing of wheat, the mining of coal or iron—and depend little upon the processing, by manufacture, of those raw materials, these natural resources are put under a severe drain to support a growing population. The income which comes to a region from cutting trees or growing cotton and bringing them to a point of transportation is only a small fraction of the income, the "value added," when those trees have been processed into paper or the cotton into overalls. If a region depends—as most "colonial" regions are forced to do— almost entirely upon the income from cutting the lumber or growing the cotton, and hardly at all upon making the paper, the textiles, the furniture, or any of the other articles manufactured from the raw resources, then the pressure to "mine" the fertility of the soil, to devastate the forests for lumber, to deplete the oil fields and coal reserves becomes very great indeed.

That pressure to deplete resources can be lessened by the growth of the industries which electric power encourages. But if the industry is only exploitative, if it does not *sustain* the productivity of the resources upon which all of us depend, industry can exhaust a region and hurt its people's chances of security and happiness. The "how" of industrial development, like the "how" of developing a river or the land or the forests, is the all-important point.

After the war great energies will be released in the development of many parts of the world. Unless a new way of thinking and acting wins support, this period of "development" will duplicate for every continent and every region the stories of modern Ducktown and of ancient Babylon.

Good will is not enough, nor speeches nor noble intentions. There will be those in abundance. There are principles and policies to develop and to observe if people are to benefit and democratic institutions are to flourish. The unity of nature's resources must not be disregarded, or the purpose for which such developments are undertaken will be betrayed as it has been betrayed before: by the way the job is done.

Chapter 7

A SEAMLESS WEB:

The Unity of Land and Water and Men

IT WAS the methods of the past which the Act creating TVA deliberately repudiated. For in this major characteristic—the unified approach—TVA was a definite break with government tradition. There was, however, nothing particularly novel about the individual tasks entrusted for execution to this new agency. There were long-established precedents for government activity in flood control and navigation, in forestry and agriculture, and in research. Public power systems were not an innovation. The new thing about the TVA was that one agency was entrusted with responsibility for them all, and that no one activity could be considered as an end in itself. Constructing dams or rebuilding soil, whatever the activity, it had to be treated as an inseparable part of a general program to promote the well-being of all the men and women of the region, whether they worked in offices, in factories, or in the crossroads stores, in kitchens or in the fields.

The jurisdiction of the TVA cut across existing lines of federal bureaus and departments. A single agency, instead of half a dozen, was to design and build the dams, buy the land, construct transmission lines, and market the power the river produced. One agency was to "envision in its entirety" the potentialities of the whole river system, for navigation, for power, for flood control, and for recreation. The contrast between such an administrative scheme for the Tennessee River and the plans on other rivers is illustrated by a contrasting instance, where one set of men designed a dam, another agency actually built it, a third group of men then took over the operation and maintenance of one part of the dam, still a fourth group another part, a fifth disposes of one share of the output—each acting under separate direction and policies, with the power of decision for the several parts of the task centered in different hands in distant places.

Each TVA dam is a project of several purposes. TVA's engineers have designed it not only to give navigation depth to the river and the greatest possible protection from floods, but to assure every other benefit, of which power production is only one. And every dam is part of a system for the whole river, from headwaters to mouth. The location, the size, the operation of each dam is determined in relation to all the others, so that the total potential value of the entire river may be realized.

It makes a great difference in the way a job is done when responsibility is as broad as that of the TVA, when the welfare of the region is the direct objective, when the construction of a dam or a series of them is seen as only one means to that end. Each task must be carried out in such a way as to contribute to that total result, to salvage every possible benefit. With this range of responsibility in mind, the Board of the TVA decided at the beginning to build the dams by "force account"—that is, that the TVA should directly select, hire, train, and supervise the workmen and be responsible for the policies governing wages and conditions of work. The almost universal federal practice is otherwise. Government construction projects are generally "let out to contract"—that is, a contractor agrees to do the job, to buy the materials, select and pay the employees, and turn over a finished job for a price. With a few minor exceptions, for work of a special and temporary nature, such as tunnel building or the raising of a bridge, every man who has worked on these Tennessee Valley projects has been employed directly by his government. All were recruited and employed by the TVA.

Building the dams has been not only a matter of digging foundations and pouring concrete so that the river might be controlled. It has also afforded an opportunity to the men of the region to learn new skills, skills that will be badly needed as industry develops in the South. As a result of apprentice training, sharecroppers have become skilled craftsmen in these ten years, and tenant farmers have learned to be mechanics. In this way the TVA has helped to add to the reservoir of trained workmen, white and Negro, who are ready to help process the raw materials of the area.

For the same reason the job of providing adequate housing for the workers at dams built at isolated points was undertaken by the TVA itself. Creative engineers, architects, and builders on our staff spent several years developing various types of low-cost housing—demountable houses, for example, houses that could be set up on one building site and then moved on to another, always with the widest general use for the region in mind. The influence of these standards of housing, by the contagion of example, upon the private housing development throughout the valley is not difficult to detect even by the casual visitor, and the designs of prefabricated, demountable, and more conventional low-cost housing that have come out of this effort have been made available and are being used by private builders over the country.

It is not for "moral" reasons or a patronizing kind of benevolence that TVA construction villages are not "wide open," as is the general custom on public and private dam-building jobs alike. It springs from the driving force of the broad purpose of regional development, from the obligation laid on the TVA to encourage the greatest use of every opportunity to benefit from participation in this job of building the region. Because of these villages TVA was once described by a visiting satirist as the "Little Lord Fauntleroy of the construction industry." What induced this remark was probably not so much watching construction workers playing ping-pong in the Community Building as it was observing crane operators spending their evenings studying blueprint reading, or seeing men climb out of a bulldozer's seat to go and read books from the library—for such a library has been made available to every construction location, however remote in the hills.

These practices are not costly even in money. For when provisions for good food and a decent place for rest and recreation are made—assumed requirements on every TVA construction job—the stage is well set for the more important conditions of an efficient job: union organizations if the men want them, the procedures of collective bargaining, and joint committees to deal with problems of project efficiency. The unit costs of TVA construction have been low compared with private and public undertakings the country over. The jobs have been done with unusual speed. Through ten years there has never been a major interruption through strikes.

Accidents have been kept to a minimum. In 1941 TVA won thirteen first, second, or third places in the annual rankings of the National Safety Council on accident frequency or severity on large construction projects.

The accident rate, the unit costs, and the records in keeping schedules are recognized measures of efficiency on such construction jobs. Responsibilities undertaken and methods developed not merely to build dams, but to build a region by seizing every opportunity that the unified way of looking at things suggests—this it is that has contributed to the efficiency with which each single enterprise has been accomplished. And when this is the way of doing the job, the by-product benefits persist long after the crews have been disbanded and the camps dismantled. It has been our purpose, by devices which I shall later describe, to weave the housing programs, the library service, and the public health facilities available to construction workers into the fabric of the adjacent community institutions, where they will remain as locally supported services long after the workers are gone.

Added responsibilities result when no single job can be considered an end in itself. For TVA this meant that we could not ignore the dislocations of men's lives which the building of such structures inevitably caused. When the swinging buckets have poured concrete in the final open "block," and the great steel gates are closed, the river's flow is stopped. What about the hundreds of farm families upon whose acres the waters will soon be creeping; what of the communities and churches and schools affected? Under the single-purpose scheme of development, private and public alike, the answer has always been and is today: "The landowners have been paid a fair price for their land, the town has been compensated for the streets that have been inundated and for the access road that is deep below the waters. That discharges our obligation. Our job was to build a dam; that job is done. We are pulling out."

Such an answer is not by any means peculiar to river development enterprises. It is the point of view customary in most industrial developments—some recent war projects furnish particularly flagrant examples—and it is the common denominator of any enterprise not governed by responsibility for a broad purpose rather than a single objective.

The TVA could not close the gates of the dam, pay off the landowners and townspeople, and call it a day. That would not do because the resources of the region—human energies included—were to be seen as a whole, and the development of a river was only a single part of the total job of regional building.

And so, when a dam on the TVA system is still under construction and long before the waters have risen, the TVA sees to it that trained men and women of the vicinage are on their way into the countryside. They examine farms that may be for sale, so that families moved from the reservoir may have disinterested and expert advice, if they ask for it, on values and locations. The expert counsel of technicians and neighbor farmers is available to those who must move; that change provides a chance for the farmer to improve his agricultural practices. Thousands of families have obtained such guidance on a great variety of matters: simple architectural plans for a new house or the remodeling of an old one on the new location, or for the building of a poultry shed; information about the electric co-operative line near by, or about a Farm Improvement Association.

The records of this "family readjustment" have been carefully kept for fifteen reservoir areas, 8,107 farm families. The general conclusions are of some interest. Almost no farmer took cash for his land and promptly yielded to the blandishments of a "gold stock" salesman. Detailed reports, based on about half the families removed from one area, indicate that approximately 70 per cent of the farm families expressed themselves as better or equally well satisfied in their new locations. The new methods of farming they have followed have shown how a better living could be made from the uplands than older methods had provided on the river-bottom farms from which they had moved.

Farms and crops are facts. But so are human emotions, and they too must be a part of the reckoning if the idea of unity is to be realized. Take the case of burying grounds, for example. A cemetery has no economic or engineering importance. But to the families whose forebears were buried there it is often a precious symbol, a symbol rich in meaning. The personal distress it would cause to have a grave submerged under 200 feet of water—this is a serious human fact. To ignore that reality would be to accept technical "progress" as cold, hard, untouched by any understanding or concern for the emotions of men. TVA moved thousands of such graves and hundreds of cemeteries to locations selected by the families or church communities. But this physical job was not enough; it was done in a way that would express respect for the feelings of those to whom these graves meant so much, though after the lapse of many years they were often quite empty. This is a detail in a huge undertaking. But I am confident that attention to this and other similar details affecting the sensibilities of men, has had much to do with the confidence in the TVA's technical leadership and in its technicians that one finds today so firmly fixed in the minds of many people in this valley.

Because of the breadth of the underlying purpose, towns were not simply paid money damages for streets that would be inundated by the waters of the reservoirs and thereupon marked off the list of "headaches." What happened in the little city of Guntersville in northern Alabama is an instance. The backwaters of Guntersville Dam would cover a number of streets in the business section of this cotton-farmer trading center. A considerable readjustment of the streets and business life of the community was inevitable. It was not easy for the city to face the change, but, long before the waters rose, TVA planning technicians were consulting with the city and state officials. Out of this consultation came a Guntersville City Planning Commission, and later a city zoning ordinance (the first in that part of the state), subdivision controls, and a major street plan. The deep waterfront at the city's center made Guntersville a port through which today large tonnages of freight pass. Under the town's new plan, the industrial uses of the waterfront are separated from the recreational uses, and this city, extending in a long peninsula into the broad blue waters of Guntersville Lake, is today one of the most attractive small cities in Alabama. What at first seemed a calamity was turned into an opportunity, and a community sense of direction has resulted that continues to bear fruit.

Chapter 8

THE COMMON PURPOSE

IN ADMINISTERING a project of such broad scope there are of course difficulties quite aside from the multiplicity of responsibilities. Not the least of these arose within the TVA when the experts who made up its staff began to work together. Technical men are rarely trained, in the schools and universities, to see the problems of the people as a whole, as the TVA was obliged to do. It will, I think, be useful to describe how TVA, by concentrating upon a *common purpose* has tried to surmount these barriers to unified development, barriers that loom in the minds of men, and particularly of those technical specialists and experts whose collaboration is essential.

The work upon which we first embarked ten years ago called inevitably for men of many different kinds of professional and technical skills: geologists, agronomists, foresters, chemists, architects, experts in public health, wild life, and fish culture, librarians, wood technicians, specialists in recreation and in refractories, accountants, lawyers, and so on. Such an undertaking, and indeed any modern technical enterprise, requires or in any event has resulted in a high degree of specialization of function.

The terms engineer or biologist or agronomist or chemist are today classifications too general to be of much meaning. In dealing with the resource of the land, for example, foresters represent one of a dozen special fields of skill whose services are required. But forestry, itself a specialization, is divided among a considerable number of even stricter specialists—tree crop experts, nursery technicians, cutting experts, and so on. And so it is with almost every one of the major fields of knowledge upon which an administrator must depend for even the basic steps of such a great change. TVA for example once had on its staff a dendrologist, a man who had spent most of his adult life as an expert in the reading of tree rings. By the examination of the rings of ancient trees he was able to throw some useful light on rainfall cycles and extreme floods far beyond the humanly recorded data on these matters. This expert saw the whole world in tree rings, almost literally. The degree of special function is not always so refined as that, but it is extreme in such a modern undertaking as TVA. The scope of TVA's effort was no less broad than the full sweep of nature and of technology; such *specialization* of function threatened the very fundamental change in point of view toward *unity* that the TVA was intended to effect.

It was clear, therefore, that we could not hope to deal with resources as a unity through modern science (itself the product of specialization) unless we could establish a basis for the unification of these highly specialized skills upon which the enterprise wholly depended. The problem of collaboration among men of highly special responsibilities is a general one, of course, and by no means peculiar to the TVA. In the steps which we in this valley have taken toward working it out, there is a clue to the ways in which in other fields, too, these spiritually disintegrating forces can be overcome.

The unification of the various technical skills was a central part of our task in the TVA, as indeed it is a central problem in modern life. The skills are not self-co-ordinating. In the selection of TVA's technical staff the importance of the expert's need for a broad view was seen. The breadth of TVA's undertaking itself made it imperative that we seek out the kind of experts who preferred to work as a part of a unified program. But even at best it is not easy for each specialist to appraise the relative importance of his own task as part of the whole picture, or its importance as compared with the tasks in some other technical branch. In fact, the desperate part of the problem, as many people have observed, is the realization of how rarely these different groups of specialists seem to care about anything beyond their own specialties.

This is not to say that specialists are narrow human beings. It is understandable that concentration and preoccupation with a particular phase of a problem breeds impatience with anything not directly in the line of vision. The more conscientious and excited the specialist is about soil chemistry, metallurgy, fish and wild life, or statistical methods, the more likely he is to see all else as an adjunct.

It is an ironic fact that the very technical skills which are ostensibly employed to further the progress of men, by the intensity of their specialization, create disunity rather than order and imperil the whole success of their common objective. Resources cannot be developed in unity until each technologist has learned to subordinate his expertness to the common purpose, has come to see the region and its problems "in its entirety."

The ways in which this diversity of special interests appeared in TVA's actual experience will illuminate the problem. Take the questions that arise when a dam is built and the waters of a huge man-made lake will soon cover tens of thousands of acres of farms, as well as cemeteries, schools, highways, parts of or even entire towns. First of all the Board of the TVA has to decide just how much land is to be purchased. From the engineers comes a map showing just where the water will extend when the dam has been closed. The land that will be under water must, of course, be purchased. There is no debate about that. But what additional land along the new shoreline should also be purchased?

The TVA's agricultural experts urge that no more land be taken than is actually to be covered by the waters. Farm land, they argue, is land on which to grow crops; all of it is needed. At once, however, the expert on public recreation is heard from; *he* urges strongly the purchase of a wide "protective strip" along the entire shoreline, which is often several hundreds of miles long. That land, he says, ought to be forever reserved for its scenic beauty, to be used for public parks and playgrounds and to prevent the growing up of private developments that may mar the beauty of the land and lead to speculative profits for a few on what should be a public benefit for all. To the agriculture expert this is nonsense; his point of view in turn is entirely unpalatable to the recreation planner.

The malaria-control expert has still another opinion; he may want dikes built to keep the impounded waters out of low, flat areas, to reduce the opportunities for the mosquito to breed, even though this requires extensive investment in earthworks and pumping equipment. In selected areas he may prefer that no one should live within a mile of the shore, so that infection may not be carried from one man to another by malaria mosquitoes. He may even insist that such an area be completely evacuated between the hours of sunset and sunrise, which is when the malaria mosquito is active. The highway engineer may have still another special attitude. He will urge, for example, that great peninsulas be purchased in their entirety and the farm families moved to other locations—this for the sake of avoiding the considerable expense of providing access highways to take the place of roads that will be flooded when the water rises.

The power expert, on the other hand, urges the most limited possible purchases of land, so that the dollar investment which his electric revenues must cover will remain at a minimum. The expert in navigation likewise will press his specialized interest; his claims to the purchases of areas to be reserved for terminal and harbor facilities or marineways may conflict with claims for the use of that same land for recreation or farming or malaria prevention. Sometimes the problem is even further complicated, as by the archaeologist, intent upon the removal or preservation of prehistoric remains in the reservoir area, or by the expert in public revenue, concerned with the adverse effect on the finances of a local government unit when certain tracts, by reason of their purchase by the government, are removed from the local tax base.

These experts, needless to say, had no pecuniary interest impelling them to insist on their various views; in that sense they were disinterested. Many of them, as a matter of fact, had come to TVA because they wanted just such an opportunity to be part of a task broader than their own special fields. Where such an atmosphere of disinterest, in a pecuniary sense, does not exist, the pressure toward "special solutions" is even further intensified.

It was apparent to us, in the case I have described, that, at first look, at least one or more of the interests were in conflict. Differences of this kind could not be intelligently settled merely by compromise between the various technicians' views, a variation of the trader's "splitting the difference." But they had to be settled; a decision had to be made. Relative dollar cost was only one factor to be considered. The final question was always this: looking at the situation as a whole, and not merely at the professional or technical standards of any one or several of the specialized interests, what course of action would yield the best results *as judged by the common purpose*, the goal of the whole undertaking—the well-being of the people of the region? The TVA experts and the Board of Directors on these occasions came together to learn from one another and merge the various special judgments into decisions of broad public purpose. The decisions made in many such reservoir cases are certainly not beyond question for their wisdom, but this at least is clear: they are products of a new kind of thinking. The problem was studied as a single problem.

With time, the barbed-wire fences began to come down within the TVA, the fences between the fields of special knowledge put up to keep one specialist out of the other fellow's domain and keep him in his own, barriers so characteristic of present-day science, of education, of engineering, even of theology. The TVA experts, themselves convinced of the value of combining their special judgments into a unified conclusion, soon developed workable methods of teamwork. It began to be taken more and more for granted (although "backsliding" was, of course, not unknown) that expertness is not an end in itself, and that each skill is only one part of the unity of knowledge necessary to do the job of developing and conserving resources.

The common moral purpose of benefit to the people, by dint of observation and participation, came to be as real to the experts as some highly technical procedure had always been. They welcomed the chance to broaden their view of their own special fields and to relate them to other areas of knowledge.

TVA's engineers, who have developed new chemical fertilizers, have no tendency today to perfect a product in the laboratory as an end in itself. They know the story of farming and the practices of farming; they are, in fact, often in the fields near by, where their products are used by farmers. And the agricultural experts have learned that the most important aid to soil rebuilding may be a device invented by the industrial engineer and marketed by a businessman. Nowadays there are fewer conflicts between experts to be settled by the Board of Directors. To most questions the specialists themselves apply the touchstone and reach a joint recommendation. An incident will illustrate my point.

When water has been backed up behind a great dam, the resulting lake offers opportunity for the malaria mosquito to breed. It increases the hazard of spreading the disease in this valley region where it is endemic. To minimize this danger and if possible to drive malaria entirely out of the valley is plainly, of course, part of the obligation of TVA, for the disease is a drain on its human resources—the South loses a substantial part of its working time to the malaria mosquito. An extensive program to this end was set up, under the direction of leading malariologists, and today it has made remarkable headway.

The malaria mosquito (*Anopheles quadrimaculatus*) deposits its larvae in the shallow water along the lake's edge. One of several methods of killing these larvae is suddenly to open the gates of the dam, and thereby quickly drop the level of the lake, leaving the larvae stranded on the shore where they will die in a day or two. But unfortunately dropping the level of the lake thus suddenly may waste an enormous amount of power that could be produced if the water were slowly fed through the waterwheels at the dam in the usual manner. The power expert objects quite naturally to "pouring a quarter million dollars worth of power down the river" as the level of the lake is suddenly dropped, by spilling water over the crest or through sluices, unused.

At the particular time I have in mind—the spring of 1942—power was desperately needed for war industries, while abnormally low rainfall had brought the river to unseasonably low levels. Unhappily it was also the season of the year that is most critical in the life cycle of the *Anopheles*, with conditions almost perfect for the larvae, and the consequences could have been grave. The situation was sufficiently important for the matter to come to the Board for consideration. But the whole case was submitted to us by only one expert, who stated that he was authorized to present the malaria as well as the power aspects of the problem. This was real progress in collaboration through the impelling centripetal force of a common unifying purpose. The malaria expert volunteered to make a day-by-day rather than a less frequent check of field conditions, a serious added burden to the members of his staff. As a consequence, however, the staff was in a position to take instant advantage of any change in the rate of mosquito breeding. Day-by-day decisions based on emergency reporting and collaboration between malaria experts, power operators, and water control engineers dissolved the crisis. The drastic draw-down of lake levels that a more arbitrary "specialist" attitude would have called for was avoided.

The crisis was met in stride; malarial hazards did not spread; little power was wasted. It was evident that the malariologists were intent also upon saving power if it could be done without risk to human life and health; they exercised their ingenuity toward that end. The power experts were likewise more interested in saving life and health than dollars, but they wanted decisions in this crisis to be based upon day-by-day facts to be sure the consequences of choice were real. I could not help recalling the early days of the Authority, with every expert fighting for his own special point of view, sometimes politely and sometimes vigorously, rarely trusting and sometimes even a little contemptuous of the specialities of other men.

I have dwelt upon the effect of the principle of unity upon the minds of technical men within the working staff of the TVA, for after all it is only through the minds and skills of men that resources can be developed, and those skills are, in these times, largely technical.

Here the men who design and build the dams, who operate the power systems, who build the terminals and roads, are working together, literally and with a conscious purpose. Their physical proximity helps. The public health physician and the many kinds of specialists are in daily touch with one another as a matter of course. They work under a single management. That helps to unify their efforts and their thinking. There would be no excuse here for such results of specialization and single-purpose thinking as Lewis Mumford refers to in *The Culture of Cities*: ". . . the paper engineer—this is an actual case," he writes, "designs an irrigation project with admirable skill in hydraulics, only to discover, after the water works have been built, that the soil is unfit for cultivation."[1] In the TVA the experts in soil are too close to the engineers for that to happen; their judgments are built into the original decisions.

A fundamental change in resource development then must begin at the beginning, *in the minds of men*, in the way men think and, so thinking, act. Because a few men began to think differently about resources a new statute was enacted, a new kind of institution, the Tennessee Valley Authority, came into being, and the thinking was on its way to an ever-widening circle—to experts, officials, and the people as a whole. For this way of thinking cannot be confined to the technical task force

[1] (Harcourt, Brace & Co., 1938) p. 375.

within the TVA. The unified development of resources must become the *common purpose*, as nearly as possible, of all the people and all the agencies of the entire valley.

This is a people's job. All the human forces and energies of the valley are essential to it. And what is true of our region is, I deeply believe, equally true of regions and people everywhere. It is just as important that a farmer upon his uplands should see this unity, as that the TVA's agricultural experts should see it. The job cannot be done unless the individual farmer, "standing at ease with nature," as Whitman said, sees his farm, his community—"the little watershed"—and the larger region all as parts of a single whole. It is quite as essential that the businessman in this valley should envision the river and the farms and the minerals and forests in their entirety as that they should so appear to the engineering forces of TVA. For a program of resource development is effective only when it is in the hands and minds of the people. The foundation of this conviction I shall seek to establish, in succeeding chapters, by calling upon the ways of this valley as supporting proof.

There is a grand cycle in nature. The lines of those majestic swinging arcs are nowhere more clearly seen than by following the course of electric power in the Tennessee Valley's way of life. Water falls upon a mountain slope six thousand feet above the level of the river's mouth. It percolates through the roots and the sub-surface channels, flows in a thousand tiny veins, until it comes together in one stream, then in another, and at last reaches a TVA lake where it is stored behind a dam. Down a huge steel tube it falls, turning a water wheel. Here the water's energy is transformed into electricity, and then, moving onward toward the sea, it continues on its course, through ten such lakes, over ten such water wheels. Each time, electric energy is created. That electricity, carried perhaps two hundred miles in a flash of time, heats to incredible temperatures a furnace that transforms inert phosphate ore into a chemical of great possibilities. That phosphatic chemical, put upon his land by a farmer, stirs new life in the land, induces the growth of pastures that capture the inexhaustible power of the sun. Those pastures, born of the energy of phosphate and electricity, feed the energies of animals and men, hold the soil, free the streams of silt, store up water in the soil. Slowly the water returns into the great man-made reservoirs, from which more electricity is generated as more water from the restored land flows on its endless course.

Such a cycle is restorative, not exhausting. It gives life as it sustains life. The principle of unity has been obeyed, the circle has been closed. The yield is not the old sad tale of spoliation and poverty, but that of nature and science and man in the bounty of harmony.

Chapter 9

DEMOCRACY AT THE GRASS ROOTS:

For the People and by the People

It is not the earth, it is not America who is so great,
It is I who am great or to be great, it is You up there, or any one,
It is to walk rapidly through civilizations, governments, theories,
Through poems, pageants, shows, to form individuals.

Underneath all, individuals, I swear nothing is good to me now
that ignores individuals. . .

—WALT WHITMAN

PEOPLE are the most important fact in resource development. Not only is the welfare and happiness of individuals its true purpose, but they are the means by which that development is accomplished; their genius, their energies and spirit are the instruments; it is not only "for the people" but "by the people."

The purpose of resource development must be more than the mere physical welfare of the greatest number of human beings. It is true that we cannot be starving and cold and still be happy. But an abundance of food, the satisfaction of elementary physical needs alone, is not enough. A man wants to feel that he is important. He wants to be able not only to express his opinion freely, but to know that it carries some weight; to know that there are some things that he decides, or has a part in deciding, and that he is a needed and useful part of something far bigger than he is.

This hankering to be an *individual* is probably greater today than ever before. Huge factories, assembly lines, mysterious mechanisms, standardization—these underline the smallness of the individual, because they are so fatally impersonal. If the intensive development of resources, the central fact in the immediate future of the world, could be made personal to the life of most men; if they could see themselves, because it was true, as actual participants in that development in their own communities, on their own land, at their own jobs and businesses—there would be an opportunity for this kind of individual satisfaction, and there would be something to tie to. Men would not only have more things; they would be stronger and happier men.

Resource development need not be held fast by the de-humanizing forces of modern life that whittle down the importance of the individual. Surely it should be freed of their grip, for they are the very negation of democracy. ". . . nothing is good to me now that ignores individuals."

It is the unique strength of democratic methods that they provide a way of stimulating and releasing the individual resourcefulness and inventiveness, the pride of workmanship, the creative genius of human beings whatever their station or function. A world of science and great machines is still a world of men; our modern task is more difficult, but the opportunity for democratic methods is greater even than in the days of the ax and the hand loom.

A method of organizing the modern task of resource development that not only will be based upon the principle of unity but can draw in the average man and make him a part of the great job of our time, in the day-to-day work in the fields and factories and the offices of business, will tap riches of human talent that are beyond the reach of any highly centralized, dictatorial, and impersonal system of development based upon remote control in the hands of a business, a technical, or a political elite.

It is just such widespread and intimate participation of the people in the development of their valley that has gone on here in these ten years past.

The spiritual yield of democratic methods, a renewed sense that the individual counts, would be justification enough. But there is yet another reason, a practical one, for seeking at every turn to bring people actively into the task of building a region's resources; there is, I think, really no other way in which the job can be done. The task of harmonizing and from time to time adjusting the intricate, detailed maze of pieces that make up the unified development of resources in a world of technology is something that simply cannot be done effectively from some remote government or business headquarters.

The people must be in on that job. The necessities of management make it mandatory. Efficiency, in the barest operating sense, requires it. There is nothing in my experience more heartening than this: that devices of management which give a lift to the human spirit turn out so often to be the most "efficient" methods. Viewed in any perspective there is no other way. No code of laws or regulations can possibly be detailed enough to direct the precise course of resource development. No district attorney or gestapo could, for long, hope to enforce such a regime. No blueprints or plans can ever be comprehensive enough, or sufficiently flexible, as a matter of management, for so ever-changing an enterprise. It is the people or nothing.

From the outset of the TVA undertaking it has been evident to me, as to many others, that a valley development envisioned in its entirety could become a reality if and only if the people of the region did much of the planning, and participated in most of the decisions. To a considerable degree this is what is happening. Each year, almost each month, one can see the participation of the people, as a fundamental practice, grow more vigorous, and, although it suffers occasional setbacks, it is becoming part of the thinking and the mechanics of the development of the Tennessee Valley.

In this and the next several chapters I shall illustrate how TVA has undertaken its job of region-building at the grass roots, and how regional decentralization is at work in almost every side of the valley's life—among farmers, workmen, businessmen, local officials, and in TVA's relations with state and local governments. In telling how these ideas have been put in practice, I have chosen to begin with the story of how TVA has applied grass-roots democracy to the job of rebuilding the land.

The farmers—there are about 225,000 farms in the watershed of the Tennessee River, with 1,350,000 people living on them—have long seen that their lands were in trouble. They knew, almost all of them, what they wanted. They knew that what was needed was to increase the productivity of their lands, to heal the gullies, to keep water on the land, and to prevent the soil from washing away. Like almost everyone else they were reluctant to change their habits of doing things. They wanted to have a say-so about changes, they had to be "shown"; but when their confidence had been earned they were enthusiastic, and they were generous of spirit.

The farm experts, both in the Department of Agriculture's scientific bureaus in Washington and in the state agencies of the Tennessee Valley, had known most of the technical answers to the *separate* problems of soils, of fertilizer, of terracing, and had known them for a good many years. They were competent in their special fields, and devoted to their work. Nevertheless farm income in the valley as in the whole Southeast continued at a low ebb; in some counties the average cash income for a farm *family* was less than $150 a year. Soil losses were appalling. Farm tenancy increased. Changes in farming favored by the technicians, away from cotton and corn, for example, did occur, but the pace was so slow that the direction on the whole continued downward. Entire rural counties, the towns included, were without a single telephone, a mile of farm electric line, a public library, a newspaper, a hospital, a single public health officer.

The technical knowledge of farming problems in the agricultural agencies, state and federal, was extensive, but it was largely generalized. It was not based on the needs of a particular farm or farming community. When this knowledge did reach the farmer, through reports of scientific results on experimental plots, in pamphlets, or by word of mouth through one of many agencies, it was usually a succession of separate bits of knowledge, and it was often remote from the farmer's individual problems. He was likely to be confused by the multiplicity of "remedies" and the more than a score of different governmental agencies with which he must deal on agricultural problems.

What was needed was not alone more technical information, but that *on the farm itself* there should be a unification of all the available knowledge and skills. The technical knowledge of all kinds available at the various state university agricultural experiment farms had somehow to be moved to thousands of valley farms, actual farms. What happened at a beautifully equipped experiment station or in a laboratory was one thing; what would happen on a man's farm was quite another. The laboratory had to be taken to the farm; the whole farm as a business was the farmer's problem.

Furthermore, as TVA saw it, and as the agricultural colleges were quick to confirm, the individual farmer was the only one who could *apply* all this available expertness. He must therefore become the center of the scheme of education in new methods. We did not want a method of restoring soil whereby the farmer would be ordered; he would learn *by doing*, on his own place; his neighbors would learn by watching him and adapting what "worked out." Nor did we want a mere false front, using the outward form of voluntary and educational methods to disguise actual coercion, or "uplift," or narrow political purposes.

After some searching the method that was worked out, with state, local, and federal agencies as co-operating parties, centered about "whole farm demonstrations" on tens of thousands of dirt farms. The results in physical terms I have already summarized. On the land of these demonstration farmers two ideas met and were combined in action: the idea of unity, and the democratic idea that much of the planning and execution of resource development must be in the hands of the people.

These thousands of typical working farms are the schoolrooms of the valley. Here farmers, their wives and children, with their neighbors learn and demonstrate the unity of resources, learn and demonstrate the principles of grass-roots democracy. Here there is brought to them the fruits of the technical man's skills. In each of the valley's counties there are one or more Farm Improvement Associations, with a total membership of more than 32,000 farmers. These associations are organized by the farmers and operated entirely by boards of trustees elected by them.

The demonstration farm program of the Tennessee Valley began, back in 1935, in this way: The farmers in a community, called together by their county agricultural agent, selected several of their own number who were willing to have their farms serve as a "demonstration" for the rest. Later on it became apparent to farmers and technicians that all the farms in a community usually constituted a more useful unit for demonstration than one farm or a scattered few. As a consequence what are called "area demonstrations" were set up by the farmers' associations. Some counties contain twenty such community-wide demonstrations, with as many as eighty families in such a single "little valley."

The hub about which these demonstrations turn is the soil mineral *phosphate*. (In some of a thousand other valleys, differently situated, the use of water for irrigation, say, or electric power might be that hub.) The technicians in the state institutions had long known that most of the valley land was deficient in phosphate; it is coming to be recognized as a deficiency of most American farming land. More than a generation ago the pioneer conservationist Charles Van Hise had said that the depletion of soil phosphates "is the most crucial, the most important, and the most far-reaching problem with reference to the future of the nation." This the technicians had long known. But the drain has gone on, at unabated pace. My associate on the Board, Dr. Harcourt A. Morgan, a leading agricultural scientist, knew more about the almost magic effect of adding this mineral to "poor" soils than any man in America. But he knew, too, and patiently taught that what was necessary was not merely adding phosphate to the soil but a change in the entire management of individual farms. In that change phosphate could be a fulcrum for other needed adjustments, a central vantage point from which to see and to learn the lesson of the seamless web.

Between the expert and the farm was a crucial gap which the methods of the past left unfilled. What TVA has done is to throw a bridge across that gap.

Furthermore TVA has brought together and concentrated upon the solution of the problems of these typical farms technical and scientific forces of every kind, and not just those usually deemed "agricultural." The inventor, the engineer, the transportation expert, and the businessman have all had a hand in the work of farm adjustment. As important as any of these "outsiders" were the chemical engineers. The adequate use of phosphate in the past had in part been impeded by its cost to the farmer. A group of TVA chemical technicians, aided by every other source of expertness in Washington and the Tennessee Valley, was set to work in 1933 to reduce the cost by producing this fertilizer in *highly concentrated form*, thereby making large savings on transportation and bagging costs.

The huge munitions plant at Muscle Shoals, inherited by TVA from World War I, became the center of technical research of this kind. By 1935 a wholly new electric-furnace phosphate process had gone through the pilot plant stage and was technically proven. TVA subsequently constructed a plant capable of producing 150,000 tons a year of new and improved plant food for the land from the fossilized bones of animals which lived in the sea that once covered middle Tennessee—for that is what phosphate ore is. The resulting granules of one form of these products were four times as concentrated as what had previously been in general use.

The state agricultural agencies and TVA, working together, showed that this new form of chemical, applied to the land, in combination with ground limestone (a cheap and plentiful rock), would enable clover and other legumes to grow where before the soil would not sustain them. These legume plants, such as clover, bear on their roots tiny nodules, rich in another element, nitrogen, drawn by the tiny bacteria in the nodules from the inexhaustible supply in the air. Three pounds of nitrogen could thus be "manufactured" out of the air, on the farmer's land, for every one pound of phosphorus he put on the soil. Phosphate and lime, through legumes, would thus add nitrogen. The three together meant a revitalized fertile land.

A soil badly deficient in these three basic elements is dead, sterile. No seed would ever grow to cover it against the six thousand tons of water that fall each winter on every valley acre. A soil rich in these elements could, with planning and with "know-how" in the farmer's hands, be made part of a valley-wide scheme to conserve the soil and the streams, and thereby to strengthen the people.

Here were new, modern technical tools: a concentrated mineral phosphate, and the experts' generalized knowledge of what science could do to help increase the productiveness of land. But it was the people on the farms who must use these tools. And to use them effectively meant that the individual farmer must plan ahead, adjust and readjust the management of his entire farm, as a plant manager must plan and readjust his whole operation to a radical new machine. It meant that in that planning he needed technical counsel, as the problems arose. He ought to have the advice of the ablest farmers in his neighborhood. Before he could "realize" on these new tools he would have to surmount all manner of barriers, physical and economic. And, finally, if the community and national interest were to be served by this technical advance, the farmer on his land must learn the truth of unity in resource development: that his farm was not only a field or two, woodland, a pasture and a house and barn, but a unit; that likewise the land and water, forests and minerals, power and industry were all inseparable parts of his own work and life; that on that farm he is part of the cycle of nature.

There, on that land, the farmer would see how science affected his own daily life. In this way the chemical plant at Muscle

Shoals, the great turbines at Norris Dam, the laboratories of the state universities, in short, the world of science, would come to have meaning to the man who after all was their "boss." Science, if brought thus close to him, would enable the average man (on a farm or in the town) to learn what it is that technology makes feasible, for him, what, in short, are *the people's alternatives*; without that knowledge what reality is there in the free man's democratic right to choose?

The benefits of such grass-roots thinking are almost as great for the scientist as for the layman. Technology is never final. What the farmers themselves observe, in the actual use of a soil mineral on their land, is of great value in laboratory research to open new doors to ever new discoveries. And this has actually occurred at TVA's Muscle Shoals plants and laboratories where farmers have stood at the elbow of chemical engineers while they designed new equipment for new products adapted to the farmers' actual observed needs. Keeping open a living channel of communication *between the layman and the technician,* a needed stimulus to science, invention, and industry, is another yield of grass-roots methods.

To return to the demonstration farm. Once selected, the first step was to map and inventory this farm schoolroom. These maps and inventories are not "documents," built up by questionnaires from a distance, nor are they "professional." They are made by the farmer and the committee of his neighbors. Then the farmer, the technicians, and the county agent and his demonstration assistant, "talk over" that map. They walk over the place, map and inventory in hand, often several times, still talking it over. A new management plan for the farm is the result, reduced to writing. In return for the use of his farm as a schoolroom and for his promise to keep detailed records so that others may profit by his experience, the demonstrator is supplied without cost (except freight) with TVA concentrated phosphate minerals sufficient to carry out the "new plan." He agrees with his neighbors to use these minerals on crops that will further the building of the soil and store more water in it, and not otherwise. For all the other adjustments he must pay his own way: the needed lime, terracing, cattle for the pasture that takes the place of the cotton field, and fencing for that pasture; the sheds and barns and necessary machinery. Most of these farmers had depended for their cash upon the soil-costly crops: cotton, corn, tobacco. They embarked upon a change that would rebuild the soil. Most of them had little if any working capital. What they put in, out of meager resources, was "venture capital," and too they risked the loss of their source of cash income to carry the family through the winter. But they tried it voluntarily, more than 20,000 of them in the states of the Tennessee Valley alone, and succeeded.

Most demonstration farmers have succeeded in increasing their capital resources, many have increased their income in cash received or in a rising family living standard; at the same time they have conserved and revitalized their soil. This is important because this method, being voluntary with no powers of enforcement in anyone, depends upon hitching together the farmer's self-interest and the general public interest in the basic resource of the soil. The individual has made himself one with the common purpose which the TVA idea holds for all individuals, the development of the resources upon which all stand. Self-interest here has served that public interest.[1]

For a time these new ways of doing things were viewed with some suspicion. All kinds of rumors spread through the countryside. One story was that, once a farmer put this TVA phosphate on his land, the land would thenceforth belong to the "gov'ment." But when on one side of a line fence there grew little but worthless sedge grass, and on the other the field was heavy with crimson clover and alfalfa, a change in attitude and interest took place. The demonstration farms became places to

[1] The operating details have been set out, and are available, farm by farm, county by county, in the records of the co-operating state agricultural extension services, not only in the Tennessee Valley, but in many states in all parts of the nation to which the demonstration programs have recently spread.

visit, to study, to emulate. The greatest effect in spreading new farming practices has been among those who have never been selected as demonstrators at all. Hundreds of farmers, non-demonstrators, will spend a day going from one of these farm schoolrooms to another.

A report from Virginia shows that large proportions of the "students" went home and adopted some or all the changes on their own farms. I have attended some of these all-day meetings where scores of farmers gathered in the fields, earnestly observing, asking questions, arguing, prodding the "experts" for an answer to this difficulty or the "why" of this or that.

Thomas Jefferson, also a Virginia farmer, saw that education is the foundation of a democratic nation; what was true in the eighteenth century is doubly true when technology of a hundred kinds must be at the hand of every citizen. At these meetings one man steps up and tells his experience; then another adds his story. One man's planning is compared with another's. The "lessons" learned are taken back to be tested at home.

At one meeting in northern Alabama, for example, three hundred farmers from eight different counties gathered on the Aaron Fleming farm in a single day's meeting. As a result of what they saw at this one session alone 150,000 acres of the land of non-demonstrators were affected; 10,000 Alabama acres were for the first time put under a protective cover of legumes against the washing of winter rains; and so on with other changes—restoring and saving soil, storing water on the land, increasing by 30 to 100 per cent the efficiency in production of once almost exhausted American soil, providing new business in the neighboring towns and cities, and in manufacturing centers far away.

First of course the farmer thought about his own land, his own family, then about his neighborhood. He began to work with his neighbors. First they concerned themselves with farming, then community forest-fire protection, then the school, the community's health problems, the church. Thus what begins as "soil building" or "better farming," by the inevitable force of unity of resources and men, soon "touches and gives life to all forms of human concerns," to use language of the President's original message concerning the TVA.

Farmers began working together, concentrating their efforts upon a matter far more important than any one man but in which each individual was deemed an essential part. The single farm demonstration developed into area demonstrations, these into county-wide associations, with trustees elected from all parts of the county. From phosphate and lime other common interests grew, such as livestock and its improvement, since without cattle and sheep no farmer could utilize the forage of his pastures and meadows.

What about refrigerating some of the meat produced on these pastures? The technical men were called upon, a simple matter since they were close at hand. Agricultural engineers worked out an answer: a walk-in locker refrigerator that would accommodate a dozen families. No fancy and expensive gadget; the experts were too close to the people to wander off into such professional perfectionism. This cooler was so simple that any community carpenter could build it at a low total cost. One was set up for a demonstration at White Pine community. It worked, was practical, became accepted, was purchased from TVA. Then it was adopted, on their own, by many communities. Hundreds of thousands of pounds of meat are being stored in them. Income increased. The diet of thousands of farmers was improved, not merely by preaching about the need but by setting the experts to work figuring out a *workable alternative* by which the people could make their choice of better diet a reality.

In much the same way a number of other technical answers which the valley's experts have devised have been tested by groups and organizations of farmers acting together: food dehydrators (a field in which the Tennessee Valley had already produced practical results before the war gave the subject such urgency); portable irrigation; a simple low-cost electric barn hay drier; new farm uses for small electric motors; a portable thresher; quick-freezing, and so on. Each of these technical efforts to make it possible for a farmer to afford doing what he wanted to do, i.e., farm so that his soil would be conserved, was tried out on actual farms by a group of farmers studying the "contraption" together, making suggestions together, and later often ordering one of the appliances from a commercial source for their own community use.

Buying feed or fencing, and selling eggs or berries or cattle, by individual farmers quite naturally gave way in many counties to group purchasing and marketing through the same association which administered the demonstrations. Today, through this natural evolution, the Farm Improvement Association has become more and more a medium for initiating many other projects for building rural life.

In the Tennessee Valley the effect of working together, building a fertile soil, and finding ways to protect it and keep it strong is not merely a matter of men's livelihood. Revitalizing the soil has done things to the people and their institutions quite as much as to the land. Schools have been painted, lighted, or rebuilt, church and community activities stimulated; the effect is felt in a score of people's activities which they share in common. Only cynics will find this surprising. To those with faith in humankind it is natural enough that when men adopt a common purpose so deep and broad as that of working with nature to build a region's resources there ensue inevitable consequences to the spirit of men. These indeed may be the most important result of all.

Similar consequences in the rural life of this valley have followed upon another fruit of technology: electricity. Here again farmers worked together, organizing their own electric co-operatives, sometimes against the opposition of private agencies. Electricity became a fulcrum, as did phosphate, for many changes. Electricity induced changes in farm management practices; soil conservation was encouraged. The portable electric motor, the refrigerator, electric cooling of milk, and soil heating by electricity meant increased farm income, and so the farmer could afford to buy more phosphate at the store, bid in more cattle at the auction, put in more grass, winter grain, and legumes, less corn and cotton.

And, as in the case of the technical lever of phosphate, electricity's part in furthering unified development of resources through human understanding went far beyond the business of making a living. The coming of electricity has had an important effect upon standards in rural schools, for example. Similarly in farm homes. When an electric range or refrigerator comes into a farm kitchen the effect is always much the same: the kitchen gets a coat of paint, is furbished up; not long after, the rest of the house spruces up; a new room is built on, pride begins to remake the place—pride supported by the added income that comes from "smart" use of electricity for farm purposes. You can follow the trail of new electric lines in many sections by observing the houses that have been thus tidied up.

When the principles of grass-roots democracy are followed, electricity, like soil minerals, provides men with a stimulus in their own lives, as well as an opportunity to work together with others toward a purpose bigger than any individual. By that act of joint effort, of citizen participation, the individual's essential freedom is strengthened and his satisfactions increased.

A common purpose furthered by grass-roots methods not only draws neighbors together in a community, then in a county and a group of counties; as time goes on the whole region, from one end to another, has felt the effect. The North Carolina farmers in the high mountains of Watauga or Jackson counties are brought closer to the Virginians and to the Alabama and western Kentucky farmers of the red clay flatlands. A common purpose is making us one valley.

Nor is this cohesive effect confined even to the Tennessee Valley. In twenty-one states outside the valley, seventeen of them outside the South, similar demonstration farms using TVA phosphate, now numbering 5,000, have been organized by the farmers and the institutions of those states and are operating along similar lines, though on a less extensive scale.

Not long ago two busloads of farmers from the great dairy

state of Wisconsin came to the valley "to see for ourselves." Something had gone wrong with their own lands. They spent days walking over Tennessee and Alabama demonstration farms. Today, in Wisconsin, TVA phosphate is being used in the same kind of demonstrations in twenty-seven counties of that state. For me one of the pleasantest experiences of these years was the sight of a Wisconsin farmer sitting on an automobile running board with an Alabama cotton farmer, both completely absorbed, talking over together their experiences with their land. Their grandfathers may have fought against each other at Shiloh. These citizens, however, would never think of Alabama and Wisconsin in the same way again. Not even the visits to the valley of hundreds of earnest "learners" from Mexico, China, Brazil, Australia, and a dozen other foreign lands has more meaning than the meeting of those two men on that Alabama farm.

Chapter 10

THE RELEASE OF HUMAN ENERGIES

THE story of TVA at the grass roots is not merely a story of soil conservation. It is an account of how through a modern expression of ancient democratic principles human energies have been released in furtherance of a common purpose.

The human energies that can build a region and make people's lives richer in the doing are not confined to any one kind or group of men. There is, essentially, no difference in this respect between farm people and industrial workers, businessmen, librarians, ministers, doctors. All who live in the valley are needed in varying degrees, in this task of resource development.

The individual satisfactions that come to a man from actively participating in such a basic undertaking are great whatever his calling. Working on one's own farm or upon a TVA dam affords such an opportunity, and so do public or private industrial research and development, or furthering the use of the new TVA-made lakes as a transportation resource. The principles of democracy at the grass roots remain throughout the same; every plan and action must meet the test of the question: Does this activity in furtherance of unified development employ *methods that bring in the people,* that give the people themselves, in this fundamental task, the fullest opportunity for the release of the great reservoir of human talents and energies?

Take, for example, the construction workers who actually built the TVA structures one sees up and down the valley. Those men have played an active and a major part in the whole task of region-building. The particular TVA methods which brought about this result, although of course quite different from working at the grass roots with farmers, are the same in principle; those methods meet the test I have just stated.

In pouring concrete so that the Douglas Dam could be built on a world-record schedule, in tending the glow of the giant electric furnaces at Muscle Shoals, or in stringing aluminum and copper cable along the line of march of transmission towers, TVA workers know, and show they know, that in thus working for their valley they are working for themselves; they build for themselves. Cheaper electricity is worth their labor; development of the valley's resources means more of the right kind of private industry—a better chance for their skills and the skills of their sons.

Since 1933 the TVA has carried on its construction work as a direct employer of tens of thousands of workers. At least 200,-000 different individual workers have done their stint in the TVA. Almost all of them have come from the Tennessee Valley. Thousands of craftsmen—carpenters, machinists, electrical workers, equipment operators, "cat" drivers, steam fitters, to mention but a few of all the skills required in such a construction job—have had a vital part in building a man-made control and plan into the flow of the river.

Many of these men have more than once in the past decade wiped their tools at the completion of one dam and a few days later laid them out again miles away or over the mountain where the next dam was going in. Some have seen their sons "learn the trade" as apprentices, and seen them take their places as full-fledged certified journeymen in the course of TVA construction. Some have seen their boys go up as foremen in their own trade. Each knows the youngster can handle the job because the apprenticeship he served was measured step by step with requirements for skill defined and taught by the proven journeymen themselves, supervised and administered jointly by their unions and the TVA management. These men and their labor organizations—nearly all of TVA's construction and operating employees are members of unions—have for years had a formal agreement with the TVA covering hours of work, wages, working conditions, the adjustment of grievances by orderly procedures, and the like. The workers' recognition of the part they play in the unified development of the valley is written into the opening words of that agreement in this language: *"The public interest in an undertaking such as TVA always being paramount . . ."*

How well labor has served the public interest, the valley's interest, as their own through the rigors and rewards of building dams, of keeping the power lines hot and the phosphate moving to the land, is written in the fastest schedules ever met for major dam building anywhere, in low costs, and in the quality of the jobs they have completed. Labor's rank and file and their chosen leaders have made TVA's business their business and hence the valley's interest their interest.

Management in the TVA takes but small credit for enlisting the active participation of organized labor in the job of harnessing the river. It was labor, almost from the beginning of the project, that saw in the TVA an opportunity to prove that the worker of the South is worthy of his hire, that he can master new skills, that good wage standards and working conditions arrived at among free men through the process of conference and collective bargaining are democracy's key to efficiency, low costs, and quality workmanship. There have been false notes occasionally, of course. In the first year or so of TVA there were those who saw in the job at the dam nothing more than a chance to get a "government job." Among the supervisors and labor representatives a handful of aspiring tough guys thought, mistakenly, that here was an opportunity to muscle in with their special brand of local racketeering. But the vast majority looked at it quite differently.

The way the workers were selected had something to do with the result. In 1933 the TVA held written examinations in 179 counties in seven states as a method of finding the few thousand recruits needed to build Norris Dam, the first of the chain. For the man whose mental processes were inclined to freeze when he had pencil and paper before him, a part of the examination was in pictures—for we were seeking mechanical aptitude and general intelligence. Thus, on a given day, some 38,000 of the original 60,000 applicants for jobs went to the school or courthouse of their county seat and did business with the TVA for the first time. It was an act of faith. No one had ever done such a thing before in selecting construction workers. But to thousands of men grimly eager to work after years of the depression, and accustomed to seeking a government job only through political obeisance or influence, the Workmen's Examination apparently seemed worth a try; maybe it meant a fair break on their merits.

TVA kept faith with them. And so well did the system work (as the carefully kept figures of statistical correlation between the examination results and subsequent job performance show) that the TVA Workmen's Examination was repeated in modified form every few years. It became a repetitive symbol of TVA as an "efficient job" and no need for "pull" to get on.

Men came from the mountains; their hill farms were left for their kinfolk to tend. From the cities down the river came the veterans of the building and metal trades. Coal miners in the Cumberland Plateau country took the examination. They had long been idle from the stalemate of a strike that left them in mining towns the operators had finally deserted. Many of them were later called to TVA work. After a few months at Norris Dam anyone could see that this was not an ordinary construction force. These TVA workers, on the job and in their union meetings, in specific ways made it known they had a stake in what the success of TVA could mean for labor and what it could accomplish for their region. The workers said they wanted training courses, for there would be other dams. Norris Dam was the beginning—if TVA made a good record there would be more dams and a valley-wide power system. They said they wanted to know more about cheaper electricity; and what was TVA going to do with the idle nitrate plants at Muscle Shoals?

The workers went about the job in a way that showed there was something big at stake. Visitors who talked with the men at work told us they could sense this underlying purpose among the men of TVA. Numerous incidents that came to light in hearings to consider job grievances revealed a deep loyalty to the expressed broad purposes of TVA. Frequently those very grievances were aired because the men believed that the public purposes of the whole project were being violated by supervisors or others; they wanted something done about it.

Other dams followed Norris, and at Wheeler Dam, at Pickwick, Guntersville, Chickamauga, Hiwassee, Kentucky, Watts Bar, Cherokee, Douglas, Fontana, and the others, the tone and tempo of the work was much the same. It persists to this day, though the men are more casual about it in 1943 than in 1933. That is easy to understand. They are a smoothly functioning organization. They know what they can do.

Nor have organized labor's interest and partnership in the development of the valley been confined to their TVA pay check. The leaders of labor who have worked alongside TVA's management have seen the scope of the TVA's ten years' efforts to uncover and try to remove the barriers standing in the way of the valley's—and hence their own—chance of a better living. Many of them know from bitter experience of the wasting farm land, of floods that devastate factories, jobs, and homes. TVA they saw as a way to rid the valley of these forces that held them back.

Around the wage conference table the intensity of this faith in the valley and labor's desire to help to build its future are repeated again and again. Once a year union officials, flanked by delegates from each of the major jobs, meet with management to work out adjustments in wages, working rules, and supplements to their basic agreement with TVA. On these occasions and in frequent joint meetings on other subjects there is everincreasing evidence that the TVA to them is more than a place to work. They show this too even in the formal briefs presented by the Tennessee Valley Trades and Labor Council, through which the fifteen building and metal trade unions representing some 25,000 employees present to management their facts, arguments, and ideas.

You hear expressions of the same attitude of participating in the job of rebuilding the valley in the numerous joint union-management committees that do the grinding detail work of the wage conference, or in the interchange that goes on in the Joint Union-Management Co-operative Committee or the Joint Union-Management Committee on Apprenticeship Training. In this complex machinery devised and formalized by joint agreement and experience is *a steady process of citizen self-education*: a learning in this way of the economics of this valley and the problems of *all* of its people, not of its industrial workers alone. As the men leave TVA jobs for private employment, many carry with them not only new skills but broader understanding.

The leaders of organized labor, as they participate in the affairs of the TVA, inject a strong note of realism into problems to be faced for the region's future progress. From the information they gain in their working partnership with the TVA they, like the demonstration farmer, carry the lessons of TVA into the daily stream of life and affairs throughout the valley. These leaders, the members of the Tennessee Valley Trades and Labor Council, are active, responsible citizens in their own communities. One, for example, is a member of the post-war planning committee of a large valley city. The problems of the industrial future of his community, as puzzled over by that committee, may well represent the problem of the valley in miniature. Another member of the Valley Council is president of the State Federation of Labor in his state, active in various public advisory committees and commissions dealing with education, industrial development, and the conservation and use of resources. The facts and alternatives facing the region as a whole which emerge from the discussions of labor and management in the TVA are enriched by the wealth of experience of these labor leaders; in turn the knowledge about the valley as a whole —its potentialities and the barriers to progress—which comes from the TVA staff in these joint conferences is bound to find its way into the deliberations and decisions in which labor leaders participate outside their activities directly associated with TVA.

The process of self-education on the part of both labor and management in the TVA has its effect in another way. TVA is required by law to pay the "rate of wages prevailing for similar work in the vicinity." Labor and management currently carry on factual field surveys; the facts so ascertained form the basis for wage negotiations once each year—to reach agreement as to what the prevailing rates are for the whole area in which TVA operates. In reaching agreement on this complex question two sharp alternatives are ever present: should wages be established on each TVA project to correspond to the rates "prevailing" in that particular locality; or should rates be adopted which will be uniform throughout the region on all TVA projects?

There is in this issue a myriad of conflicting interests within the ranks of labor itself—locality versus region, locality versus locality. But the give and take of discussion in the first wage negotiation, and every year since, has established a policy of viewing *the region* as the "vicinity." Labor as a whole obviously gains something in supporting this policy. But it also loses something in specific communities, because the TVA prevailing rate, while not the lowest, is not the highest or even a mathematically perfect average. And in such a process the participants on both sides of the table have learned to test the interpretation of the facts and the wisdom of their judgments by this measure: what is the answer that will best serve the *whole region*, promote the efficiency of the TVA, encourage labor standards that will aid the development of the region as a whole.

In mid-September of 1943 the Board of Directors and staff of the TVA held an all-day session with the Executive Committee of the Valley Trades and Labor Council. Not, however, to consider wages and hours; these were not dealt with at all. What was discussed in detail were problems of after-the-war demobilization; the intricacies of the freight rate differentials between the Southeast and other interior regions of the country and the East; the future fertilizer and land program of the valley.

These are not "labor" issues. They are problems of common interest to labor as to businessmen and to farmers, and because all three groups have a rising concern for the development of their valley the wise handling of these problems constitutes a bond between farmers, businessmen, and labor.

The workers of the Tennessee Valley do not need to be urged to apply their labors and pledge their faith to the rebuilding of the region, for this simple reason: *they want to live here.* Many of them have lived for varying periods in the congested industrial cities of the North, the East, and, more lately, the West. They have been in the "big money." Frequently in the past there has been no other choice but to stay away after such a periodic migration out of the South. But in ten years they see that a change has taken place in the valley. They want to live here, do their work here—these men, bred to the ridges, to the slopes and open lands of a beautiful valley, and to the ties of long established kinship in their communities and in their cities. And a man's wish to be in one place and not another must be respected as a basic fact in any democratic planning.

The methods of TVA, working at the grass roots, apply to businessmen as well as to farmers and to labor. The changes in this valley within the decade have been due, to an important extent of course, to businessmen. Although many at first were suspicious of TVA, or saw it only as a power producer or a form of "politics," by the end of the first decade most businessmen have accepted as their own the TVA idea of region-building quite as wholeheartedly and understandingly as have farmers and industrial workers. The way in which methods of management have been developed by the TVA at the grass roots to meet some of the problems of businessmen, and to enable them to contribute to the unified development of resources, has had a great deal to do with this acceptance.

What is most encouraging to me is the unmistakable evidence

that many businessmen now think in terms of the unity that
seems to me so essential: unity of all resources, and unity in
developing them as between farmers and businessmen. And
they are becoming articulate about it, able in informal ways to
express the "lessons" we are all learning in the now mature
experiment in democracy that is the TVA. I have before me a
half-page newspaper advertisement of the Alabama Dairy
Products Corporation that is an unpretentious but genuine illustration of what I have in mind. Five years ago this business
was set up in the small city of Decatur, Alabama, by local capital
and local management to build and operate a cheese factory, the
first in all northern Alabama. The ad begins in large letters:

THE CHEESE PLANT
IS A
CHILD
OF THE PEOPLE AND
TVA . . .

TVA brought new hope to the farmers who were struggling with
the washed, worn-out lands. The Authority's wide erosion control
plan combined with an intensive soil rehabilitation program resulted
in richer farming lands.

Then electricity came to the farm, lighting the way to a wide diversification program. This electric power was to aid the farmer to
expand into branches other than the production of one major crop.

Following expert advice the farmer now began to build a fine dairy
herd. Steadily it developed to the size which demanded a ready market for the product.

Here is where the cheese plant began . . .

Businessmen and business enterprise have come to understand
to a remarkable degree the principles of interrelation upon
which, under the TVA idea, everything depends. An instance
is that of a large manufacturer producing paper from wood
pulp. In this operation immense quantities of water are used,
drawn from one of the mountain tributaries of the Tennessee.
The company was put to considerable expense in processing

the 45,000,000 gallons of water it used each day to remove the silt that drained into it, borne from the farm lands of the watershed.

Near this plant was a farm "area" demonstration. The company's officials began to observe that the water flowing to the streams from these phosphate-using farm lands contained less silt than before, because of the improved crop cover over their slopes, and that the flow of water was more nearly equalized. If the farmers on the watersheds from which the company obtained its own supply of water could adopt the methods used on these area demonstration farms, it might so reduce the silt in the water as to eliminate these expensive desilting operations. Therefore these businessmen offered financial assistance to set up area demonstrations; they became members of the Haywood County Mutual Soil Conservation and Land Use Association. Recently I attended a meeting held on several farms of the associations of the area, with a membership of six hundred farm families. Standing under the hot August sun, taking an active part, examining a field of clover or bluegrass pasture with the farmers, was one of the company's officers.

The "sights" of businessmen had widened. But so had the understanding of farmers grown, as a result of their new associate from business. They learned how important their farming practices might be to an industry where many of their sons and neighbors are earning their living.

To strengthen the opportunity for a particular kind of businessmen *to make a profit* is sometimes the best way to induce their enterprise to add its part to the unity of resource development. The valley's development of a new invention, a pressure cooker for obtaining oil from the seed of the cotton plant, is an illustration.

There are in the South some 420 mills for the extraction of oil from cottonseed, most of them small in size and locally owned. Their purchases of cottonseed from the gins, and the methods of marketing the cottonseed meal left over after the oil is pressed out, exert an influence on cotton agriculture and on the fortunes of all who depend upon cotton for a livelihood. Despite the present shift away from cotton production, cotton continues to be a southern staple, and is bound to be such for many years to come. Here again is the seamless web, for soil fertility in parts of the South is in a measure dependent on the success of the cottonseed oil industry. If the meal left over after the oil is pressed from the cottonseed could be fed to livestock in the South, as much as 80 per cent of the fertilizing value of the meal would be returned to the soil rather than continuously drained from the soil by export. And export has long been the general rule. If the operators of cottonseed oil mills in the Southeast made money, so that the meal could be produced locally and consumed locally, the whole region would benefit. Soil fertility in this case depends in part upon businessmen.

The businessmen in the cotton oil industry have had a hard time. Hundreds of the small mills have been operating for years at a very low rate of return, just hanging on. Before TVA the equipment used in the extraction of cottonseed oil had not been improved for over forty years.

The valley's technicians in the TVA and the University of Tennessee, and businessmen represented by two of the cotton oil industry's associations, after several years of work invented a cottonseed pressure cooking device, a radical improvement in the technical processes of this business. The invention is owned by a public agency; the machinery is made, under license, by several well-known machinery plants; the device has been installed in a number of cottonseed mills throughout the South. By aiding business to secure a better margin of profit, this machine gives an added opportunity to aid soil fertility and thereby the region's over-all development.

Wood-using industries furnish another instance of businessmen turning to public technical agencies that work at the grass roots. The men in this important business are finding that they can turn to the Authority's area-wide inventory of forest resources to learn the location, kind, and quantities of timber stumpage, prices, stocks on hand, and other factors affecting profitable production. A manufacturing concern, for example, asked for recommendations as to the location of an additional plant for the making of hickory handles to fill a large Army order. The TVA staff report was detailed and specific, and its recommendation took into account the use of timber by already existing wood-using operations. Thus the new plant location would fit into present business arrangements, and yet not put too severe a drain on the available standing hickory. The plant, now operating, was located in accordance with this recommendation.

These businessmen put reliance upon this counsel because, for one thing, it showed an understanding that businessmen must make a profit. And yet from the point of view of the region's resources the recommendation was sound. A good market was developed for a hitherto unmarketable species of timber. The development of the valley's resources was helped. Another group of businessmen was drawn into the task of unified development. Similarly, a new device is in the pilot-plant stage for making laminated flooring (something like the familiar plywood) out of types of lumber that heretofore were "culls." Thus first-class timber is conserved, and the foundation is being laid for what may be a profitable hard-wood "prefabricated" flooring industry.

But of course the effort to draw businessmen into the task of unified development is no more uniformly successful than would be the case with any other group. The development of traffic on the Tennessee River illustrates how businessmen have become part of that aspect of the valley's changing life; it also serves to illustrate some of the difficulties that lie in the path of grass-roots democracy.

America's inland waterways have been used extensively only by a relatively few large shippers of such commodities as coal, oil, sand and gravel, and wheat. This traditional and important kind of traffic alone would not aid greatly in developing the whole valley, and particularly its manufacturing opportunities. What is specially needed is the smaller shipper, who could not use a whole tow of barges or even a whole barge—the shipper of manufactured or partly processed articles, such as baking soda, cotton textiles, fertilizer, automobiles, flour, radios, furniture.

How could this objective be reached? One way to promote shipping on the river would be for the TVA itself to promote and develop such traffic. This would mean sending a corps of TVA traffic experts directly to prospective shippers to solicit business for the river. That method was rejected, for the grass-roots principle dictated another course, and the one that was followed. If businessmen would accept the function and responsibility of promoting the use of the river, dealing directly with prospective shippers, this would draw into the development of this regional resource a whole new group of private citizens, and give them the compensation of direct participation in their region's building.

A number of businessmen who had understood for many years how the river would further their own interests were encouraged to take the leadership. A private organization, the Tennessee Valley Waterway Conference, was formed. This association and TVA technical experts developed plans for a series of terminals physically tying the railroads and truck highways into the waterways—the first system of public-use terminals on any of our inland waterways. These would open the river to the smaller shipper who could not afford to erect his own terminal. TVA secured an appropriation from Congress for the construction of these facilities.

Thus it was the businessmen of the Tennessee Valley who became the most active participants in the development of the river's navigation. In studying whether this or that article was suitable for river movement, wide fields of education were opened. Businessmen came to discuss many matters with TVA's staff—not only its navigation experts, but inevitably industrial, railroad, agricultural, chemical, and other specialists. It was soon clear that more than transportation rates and savings were involved in the use of the river.

The river became a kind of schoolroom, too, like the demonstration farm, this time principally for businessmen, a schoolroom in the unity of resource development. Minerals and forests and the products of the farm were seen in specific cases to be interrelated closely with industry and transportation. The river, like phosphate and power, became a stimulus to a new kind of thinking, and that thinking bred new factories, new industrial ideas, and the further release of creative human energies. The pride and satisfaction which the leaders in the Waterway Conference derive from thus performing a public service is not the least important result.

This story, I have said, also illustrates one of the difficulties of TVA's methods—and there are many. In Knoxville, Tennessee, one of the largest of the river communities, local business leadership seemed apathetic. Yet it was important to the whole region that a terminal be built and used at this point, especially in war time. There was a considerable temptation for TVA not to wait for community initiative to develop, but to go ahead on its own, developing the traffic which we were sure would be available. But our whole experience made us realize that this method would prove far less effective than citizen participation.

Unless the businessmen of the community would participate, we did not believe there would be traffic through the terminal sufficient to justify the use in war time of the critical materials required in its construction. We decided, therefore, that the construction of a terminal at this one point should be deferred indefinitely. This action created considerable indignation against the TVA in some quarters of the community.

The businessmen of Knoxville, however, saw the point at once. They organized a committee, and called meetings of manufacturers and other prospective shippers. At the first of these meetings one of the local committee members, a banker, summed up the situation by this comment, as quoted in the press: "I don't believe but one thing was responsible for the apparent apathy—we looked on it like Christmas. Santa Claus was com-

ing. There wasn't anything to do but hang up our stocking and
we wouldn't do that until the night before Christmas." The
services of the president of the Waterway Conference, a resident
of another city, were requested and gladly given. TVA's staff
assistance was, of course, made available and fully used, on a
host of technical questions. The report of this citizen committee
showed that a volume of prospective traffic had been found and
developed by the committee clearly beyond anything TVA's
own staff could have produced.

It would have been simpler and easier, and would have involved less unpleasant recrimination, if TVA had accepted the
role of a bureaucratic Santa Claus. But the results, simply in
terms of economic effect alone, would have been less effective.
Democratic methods are not only right in human terms; they are
the most "efficient."

This terminal has since been built, as well as those at three
other points. After the war the TVA proposes to turn over their
operation to some kind of valley-wide non-federal public association, thus clinching further the methods of businessmen participation.

Democratic methods are often slow. Sometimes they strike
a stone wall of inaction, where other methods would seem to
yield quick results. But the benefits of such "action" by nurse-
maid or dictatorial practices are usually temporary, and often
more apparent than real.

Chapter 11

THE DECISIONS OF BUSINESSMEN

THE decisions of businessmen have never been so important as today. The way businessmen think and act in respect to the resources upon which we all depend, the way in which they use the modern skills of experts, in short the breadth of their statesmanship, will determine the future of our resources and thereby the fate of many millions of human beings.

The fate of private industry as we have known it may be at stake as well. Eloquent orators and the message of full-page advertising extol the advantages of private industry in vain if industry loses the confidence of the people. And that confidence will almost surely be forfeit if in the coming decade the people believe the results of industrialization are bad when they think there is a way that they could be good.

One has only to live as I do in a valley that is still relatively undeveloped industrially to realize how great is this gamble of the future. Looking upon the magnificence of this natural beauty you cannot fail to reflect upon what a needlessly ugly, wasteful mess industrialization has brought to many other once lovely and livable countrysides—on the Monongahela and the Tyne, the Delaware and the Ohio.

With the eyes of industry now upon this valley (as they are indeed upon many valleys the world over) planning a considerable industrial expansion here after the war, there is an opportunity to plan and to build so that our resources will endure, our natural beauty be spared despoliation. Here there is a chance to see to it that human well-being in city and town will not, through

lack of ingenuity and foresight, be needlessly sacrificed. Shall
we succeed? Is the only choice one between pastoral poverty
and industrial slums? Can private industry utilize these resources, at a profit, and yet sustain their vigor and longevity?
Can business and the common weal both be served? To be able
to make an affirmative reply is a matter of the greatest moment.

In the Tennessee Valley the answers will turn to some extent
upon how successful the TVA is in its efforts to weld a union of
the public interest and the private interests of businessmen. We
appear to be uncovering and developing in this valley principles
and practices for effecting a jointure of public interests with
private, by methods that are voluntary and noncoercive. Our
actual experience is unpretentious as measured by the scope of
the problem, but it is definitely encouraging and of not a little
significance for industry and the people of the country generally.
Although touched on in preceding chapters, it deserves more
precise discussion.

What the TVA, in specific ways, has sought to do can be
simply stated: to accept an obligation to harmonize the private
interest in earning a return from resources, with the dominant
public interest in their unified and efficient development. The
method—and this is the distinctive part of the experiment—is
to bring to bear at the grass roots the skills of public experts
and administrators not for negative regulation but *to make
affirmative action in the public interest both feasible and appealing to private industry.* By public interest I mean the interest
of people—people as human beings—not "the people" in their
institutional roles as wage earners or investors or voters or
consumers. "Underneath all, individuals," men and women and
children.

These technical skills can be most effective in promoting the
people's welfare when they function close to the conflicts between private and public interest at the time they occur and
before they become hardened and confused by the dogmas
that flourish under absentee administration. Herein lies the
reason for the productive results thus far obtained, and the

favorable prospects for the future. The real tests of the method still lie ahead; this I fully realize. The problem confronting us is complex in the extreme, and of great magnitude.

To process the raw resources of nature is a major job of private industry. For industry to be able to do the job, the people must pay to industry for that task all of its costs, including an adequate profit. Those resources, however, are the total of the people's physical substance, so if they are wasted, or spent with no thought of the future, the people are insolvent and stranded. A civilization is only strong and long-lived to the degree that it shows skill in sustaining the life and productivity of its resources. From this law of history there is no escape by the chanting of political or business catch-phrases. These are bed-rock realities.

Good, prudent management of resources by industry is a matter of national life and death. But it cannot rest upon industry's good intentions alone. Private industries are rarely either in a position (this is often overlooked), on their own, to see specifically what is needed to protect the basic public interest in resources, or able, as an industry, to take action that will protect that interest. And yet when from time to time it fails to do so we all "cuss out" industry, often in a fine frenzy of self-righteousness. As a remedy legal punishment is imposed. This is usually a judgment based on hindsight; it assumes that industry knows how to protect the general public interest. A recently added remedy has been to impose some form of regulation, almost invariably static and negative.

An industry may well have the keenest desire to maintain the people's resource solvency and their long-term interest; but what it may *want* to do and what it feels *able* to do as a private industry are often quite different things. The two interests often clash, or appear to do so. It is to this task of harmonizing such conflicts that TVA's efforts have been directed.

An important illustration is the TVA's extensive program of phosphatic fertilizer research, production, and demonstration. I have already related how the continual and alarming decline of phosphate in American lands led TVA, at its Muscle Shoals laboratories, to develop a new kind of electric furnace process. That process produced a highly concentrated phosphate fertilizer—what the technicians call a "plant nutrient." There was no doubt that the products of TVA's plant were technically superior; furthermore, this mineral upon which life depends was provided by TVA in the most effective form for use. But rock phosphate—the raw material—is exhaustible, and when exhausted is irreplaceable. With this new electric furnace not only high-grade ore deposits but also the hitherto wasted low grades could be drawn upon. This was in the long-time interest of our phosphate reserves, of the land, of the production of nutritious food, and hence of the vigor and permanence of our civilization.

The TVA was hopeful that the private fertilizer industry would adopt these technical improvements. Thereby lower grade ores would be utilized; higher concentrations would reduce transport and other costs of getting fertilizer to the land. We envisaged, as a consequence, expanding farmer demand, and a resulting large increase in private production and distribution. Thus the present woefully limited use of phosphate on the land could be multiplied and both private and public interests could be served.

The fertilizer industry, however, with some exceptions, was not convinced. Its position in 1934, at the beginning of TVA's work, was substantially this: However desirable it might be for the land and for the husbanding of ore reserves to produce concentrated phosphate, with admitted savings in cost, farmers simply would not use it. "In the past we have tried to get them to buy 'high-analysis' (i.e., concentrated) fertilizer," the industry said, "but they don't want it; what they want is the mixed and low-analysis fertilizer. And what the customer wants we must supply."

TVA obtained the best technical advice in the country, from the federal Department of Agriculture, the state agricultural institutions, and private consultants. We concluded that by actual test, demonstration, and proved results, farmers could be persuaded to use concentrates.

The story of the successful valley-wide (later nation-wide) educational program to test and demonstrate to farmers the value of concentrates I have already told. Following upon these demonstrations in twenty-eight states and the nation-wide program of the Agricultural Adjustment Administration, the sale of concentrated fertilizer produced and distributed by private industry rose sharply.

In 1934 the country's private industries produced 2,984,549 tons of phosphatic fertilizer. Five years later, in 1939, this had increased to 3,953,694 tons, while in 1942 the production reached 5,144,484 tons. In 1940 private industry sold and distributed in the valley states 40 per cent more of its phosphate product than in 1934. In the counties of the Tennessee Valley the rate of increase in use of phosphatic fertilizer, purchased by the farmer with his own funds from regular channels, was 500 per cent greater than in the country as a whole. Heretofore no such increases had ever taken place in the production and sale of this private industry's product. A report from Alabama Polytechnic Institute shows that in ten Alabama counties where demonstrations of TVA concentrates were conducted 9,071 tons of privately produced phosphate was purchased by farmers; in ten representative counties in which no demonstrations were conducted private industry sold only 830 tons. A report from a Virginia state agency makes the following statement:

In the beginning, only the demonstrators used phosphate, that supplied by the Tennessee Valley Authority. Then, as their results were observed, other farmers began to buy phosphate from dealers. . . . One concern, which has six affiliated stores in the valley area, sold 60 per cent more superphosphate during the 1937-40 period than during the preceding four years.

As such results from these demonstrations came in, the manufacturers of fertilizer ingredients, for the most part, assumed a friendly attitude toward the TVA's work. We made our technicians available to industry for counsel. A few electric furnaces were installed by private concerns, with the benefit of TVA designs. The flow of results secured the approval, too, of the national and state farmers' co-operative associations that sell fertilizers. But opposition at every step has come, with a few encouraging exceptions, from the makers and the distributors of "mixed" fertilizers, the older low-analysis material. The use by farmers of concentrates—high-analysis material—calls for changes in the present costly methods of *distribution*. This may account for the opposition, by fertilizer "mixers" and thousands of middlemen. But in public the arguments are largely in the familiar abstract phrases: "government in business," "invasion of the field of free enterprise." Neither farm organizations nor Congress has been impressed by the distributors' reasons for opposing TVA's program.

The increase in commercial sales of concentrated phosphate has been considerable. They are but a fraction of what they would be, to the great good of the land and the people who consume its crops, if in the industry there were not such a strong resistance to private expansion of facilities for the production of concentrates. This is difficult to understand, in the face of the constantly increasing demand from farmers. But, like the private electrical industry some years ago, most of the distributors (except the co-operatives) seem slow to recognize that it is in expanded production and sales, at consequent lower unit costs, and not in small production at high costs and high prices that its real interest lies.

The distributors' trade association argues that there is already as much phosphate as farmers want and need, a note out of harmony with the principles of progressive American business enterprise. Actually the country's production facilities for phosphate are wholly inadequate for the need and the demand. Since the public interest in the land and in its phosphate ores is at stake, this out-moded business policy will surely one day be replaced, as it is being replaced in the electric industry, by one that is more realistic.

The difficulties of collaboration with the fertilizer mixers and distributors have not been typical of our experience. In most cases industry has joined with us actively and with ingenuity in seeking in specific cases a way by which its own limited but important business interest could be furthered by a use of resources that is in the broad public interest. A comprehensive and unique contract between the TVA and the Aluminum Company of America illustrates how far businessmen, even those whose point of view is generally widely different from that of the TVA, will go in this direction.

The Aluminum Company has long owned several dams at the headwaters of the Little Tennessee River, a tributary of the Tennessee. Those dams, lying above the many dams of the TVA, if operated as part of the TVA system of dams, would result in greater public benefits both in power and flood control than if they continued to operate independently. The purpose of the years of study and negotiations that resulted in the contract was to find a way whereby the maximum public usefulness of the river's water resource could be secured without reducing the power available to the company from its dams or increasing its cost. Under the contract, signed in 1941, the Aluminum Company agreed to turn over to the TVA, indefinitely, the right to direct just how Alcoa's dams should function, that is, when water should be stored from hour to hour, and when released through power turbines or sluice gates. The contract's effect (without any change in Alcoa's title to its property) is to unify the control of water of the entire watershed, and thereby increase the public benefits accruing in power, flood control, and navigation. The added power benefits created by the arrangements are divided between the parties to the contract by a formula which both sides believe advantageous. A strategic power site, long owned by the company, is also turned over to TVA, and upon it Fontana Dam is now rising.

The Aluminum Company of America and TVA are organizations widely apart in their purposes. And yet by keeping their attention on the physical facts—that the river could be made more productive if Alcoa's private dams and TVA's public ones were operated as a unit—agreement was reached in a complex situation. By avoiding the conventional abstractions and clichés that usually mark discussions where public and private interests and philosophies appear to conflict, it was here possible to promote both private benefit and the people's interest.

The benefits of such collaboration by TVA with business are not, of course, confined to industry that operates for profit. Chickamauga Producers, Inc., a farmers' non-profit co-operative, is a new private enterprise which illustrates the same methods. That farmers should have a better market for strawberries was the starting point in TVA's interest in encouraging the development of this business. Why strawberries? Because it is a crop that on certain of our valley lands furthers soil conservation— the reason for TVA's interest—and at the same time can be made to provide a good cash return to farmers. But the crop was only practical for these farmers if they were not forced to "dump" the harvest on the market at one time at ruinous prices. Freezing or otherwise preserving the berries was one technical possibility that could bring soil conservation and private interests, i.e., good prices for berries, into union.

Technical research, by the TVA and the University of Tennessee, working together, resulted in a new kind of quick-freezing process and machine. The operation of the invention was taken over in 1939 by a new industry organized by the farmers who raise the berries. Other products—beans, peaches, fish—and other processes have since been added. The enterprise is on the way to financial success. In 1943, after declaring a 6 per cent stock dividend, it distributed the balance of its net income, nearly $15,000, to its farmer owners. More than three million pounds of fruit and vegetables will be packed during the current year (1943). An additional plant, costing $50,000, was built this summer. Employment in the plant is furnished to many people in the five-county area. The new technical achievement—the quick freezer—has started a business that has resulted in doubling the income from the strawberry crop.

There is still another kind of clash, or *apparent clash*, between private interests and the public as a whole. I refer to that between industry and the people as consumers of industry's products. And just as we have generally taken it for granted, that industry is *able* to determine what is the best use of resources, similarly we have uncritically assumed that each individual industry or business is in a position to determine what are the genuine needs of the consumers of its products.

There is prevalent an idea, often mistaken, that the needs of consumers will be met by industry quite automatically. Customers, so the idea runs, hold a kind of daily plebiscite. If sales fall off, that proves that the particular product or service does not fulfill the public's needs; if sales rise, that establishes that they do. Such a referendum is supplemented, of course, by customer advertising, and by many devices that induce people to "vote right" on a product.

The theory, from time to time, breaks down badly. A case in point is the way in which phosphate supply has failed to keep up with the needs of the land and of farmers. Then too we learn from time to time that new or better products are kept off the market or long delayed in order to protect the position of an individual industry. We sometimes see that the customer has no way of knowing what kind or variety of products could be produced, and therefore that he is forced to state his wants only in the terms of his ignorance of what he could get if he had a real choice (not unlike a "free" election where one may vote as he pleases so long as it is for the one candidate who is "eligible"). Or we learn that monopoly keeps a new enterpriser from supplying essential needs, or that the customer is misled or "high-pressured." The remedies, usually applied in anger, are sporadic criminal indictments, negative regulation, the everlasting "don't do it again."

In contrast with such remedies are TVA's methods of collaboration with industry to aid it in ascertaining and meeting genuine consumer needs. The story behind a new industrial product put on the market in the late summer of 1943, a kitchen-type dehydrator for home garden products, is an illustration.

On July 8, 1943, the War Production Board announced that

a number of manufacturers, almost all of them relatively small and new in the field of home appliances, had been authorized to use critical war materials sufficient to produce several thousand of such units specifically for the southeastern market. This particular home unit dehydrator has been designed by technicians of the TVA and the University of Tennessee. Behind this new device were several years of TVA research in dehydration and other methods of food preservation. The object of that research was that this region should make the most of its food-growing resources, and minimize waste. To do the job more than a technical report was needed. A home dehydrator had to be invented which private industry would consider profitable to produce and distribute. It must, moreover, be so designed as to meet the genuine needs of the people who were to use it; it must be simple in operation, effective and scientific in its results, low enough in cost so it could be sold at a price people felt they could afford.

The physical research problems presented the least difficulties. A practical method, too, had to be devised so housewives could be taught to operate the equipment with success. This was something that could not be left entirely to "salesmanship," in the customary sense.

These of course were not problems that inventors in a laboratory or sales managers in a remote office could solve. The TVA, with the University of Tennessee co-operating, turned to state agencies with which they had worked on so many other problems, agencies close to the daily life of the people. Through these local channels the facts affecting the dehydrator's design came directly from the region's kitchens to the technicians working over their models. And, through the same public local agencies, schools in the teaching of dehydration methods were organized. One, held in Knoxville in February, 1943, was attended by 150 teachers from ten states of the South; they went home to instruct thousands of others. This region is on the way to a widespread knowledge of food preservation.

The relation between industry and the Tennessee Valley's public technical agencies, of which this story is a recent instance, was dramatized in a series of conferences in the TVA's offices. Thus, in July of 1943, a manufacturer of this equipment sat across the table from representatives of the technical staffs of TVA and of the state universities of Tennessee, Georgia, Alabama, and Virginia. At his right sat representatives of the various electric power boards of the valley, men familiar with the problems of the distribution of home appliances in this particular region; they were there to speak for wholesalers and retailers of the equipment. The manufacturer stated that he would manufacture the equipment as the public agencies had designed it. He also adopted as his own a descriptive advertising sales booklet and the instructions to the consumer that were to go with each dehydrator, just as they were prepared by the representatives of the public's technical agencies. It is apparent that this industrialist saw the practical value to him of having the counsel of disinterested technicians who had channels to the consumers which he did not and perhaps could not have. He even consulted the group on the retail price at which they thought the equipment ought to be sold.

Whether or not this product ultimately proves to be a success —it is still too early to judge—is not the point. The principles the case illustrates are clearly sound. For here is a method of bringing together the initiative of businessmen and the technical judgment of agencies in close touch with the consumer viewpoint. Such a union is greatly needed.

It is because working at the grass roots has developed channels of communication with the people and their institutions that these technical services have a special usefulness to industry. Most manufacturers are thoroughly competent on their own to produce almost any kind of industrial product. Not all of them, by any means, however, are in a position to ascertain the best use of resources as judged by the over-all public interest, and most of them cannot get so close to actual consumer needs as even the promotion of their own interests as manufacturers would make desirable. Thus the ablest agricultural machinery concern did not create a thresher for grain farming in this Appalachian Mountain country, for example, because, in part, their technicians had no intimate knowledge, or "feel," for our special farming conditions and no confidence that there was a profit to be made from such a product.

Because TVA had such knowledge and such confidence it was able some years ago to design a successful portable thresher for use under such conditions in this valley. The design was adopted and is being produced and sold by a private concern. And so it has been with a good many other items of equipment now in private production and sale.

Through all the examples I have been reciting, of planning by democratic and voluntary methods, runs the theme and purpose of bringing into union two vital concerns: the compelling necessity that our natural resources be made sustaining and permanently productive for everyone's welfare, and the business necessities of private industry.

Chapter 12

EXPERTS AND THE PEOPLE

THE TVA's collaboration with industry is based upon the use of technical skills in the public interest, the skills of public and private experts.

Such a conception of public-private collaboration sometimes meets with a cool, not to say hostile, reception. This will almost invariably occur where a particular industry clings to the traditional idea that "co-operation between business and government" means that the function of public agencies is to accept and bless all of industry's existing policies even if thereby resources are misused. That is not the reaction of responsible fellow worker, but of a yes-man.

Around such a mistaken notion of "co-operation" a whole philosophy and practice in business and government has grown. It has, for example, led trade associations and industries into the ambiguous practice of taking a public official directly out of government service and making him their government "contact" man in order that the relations with government will be "friendly." This erroneous idea of co-operation has likewise led to the deliberate practice of buttering susceptible public officials —both the senile and the young—plying them with flattery, using elaborate publicity build-ups that describe them as "statesmen," and in other ways feeding the personal vanity and ambition of men in government.

In the short run this has had occasional success with men in the public service who are unable to distinguish between deference to themselves and deference to the responsibility that, temporarily, has been entrusted to them. But on the whole this practice—and all the other expressions of this variety of co-operation—has injured business. To the public it has seemed a betrayal of their interests. It is an invitation to the demagogue, the political baiter of business. It creates a political issue out of what is often simply a problem calling for the practical use of technical knowledge.

Some of the methods of the liberalism of 1904, now embraced too by many conservatives, for example the idea that government has only the role of an impartial referee pulling contestants out of clinches and calling fouls, are wholly inadequate today. Government is not simply an umpire, nor is it a combatant. The technical services of the government have a *job* to do—for business, for labor, for consumers, for the sustained productivity of all of us.

This point is sharpened by an interesting recent development in the TVA. One of the country's largest national distributors of goods to consumers, dealing in hundreds of thousands of articles and with the thousands of manufacturers that produce them, consults frequently with the TVA about sales and production problems as they concern the Tennessee Valley. This firm is engaged in a detailed analysis of the post-war American market. Inventions that are on their way through the laboratories and pilot plants of the TVA and its co-operating agencies, the specific needs and desires of valley users of all kinds of products —these are the subject of a steady interchange of ideas. Between merchandiser and TVA all manner of questions are passed back and forth. Does TVA see a market for a new kind of metal pleasure boat for the "Great Lakes of the South"? How does a kitchen-type flour mill stand up under the company's tests and market surveys? Does the company think the TVA's laminated flooring, made experimentally from previously unmarketable lumber, meets the price requirements of wide distribution?

The experience and realism of the company's technicians and the broad point of view of the region's experts, concentrating as they do on matching resource development with the people's genuine needs, have thus far admirably supplemented each other. In these joint conferences none of us have ever heard any of those abstract discussions which consume so much of the energy of some businessmen and politicians about "the invasion of private enterprise." The two kinds of experts have each a different function to perform, but each recognizes the place and importance of the other.

The methods TVA is developing have aided in the creation of new private enterprises, especially *small* business ventures. Mr. Paul G. Hoffman, Chairman of the Committee for Economic Development, has said that the large businesses already "have the resources and the technical ability," but it "has been too tough for small businesses to be born of late." TVA-sponsored inventions have resulted in the creation of new small business concerns, and have led to the expansion of others.

In the war period small business undertakings have suffered heavy casualties. Those who believe with Mr. Hoffman that "small business is the bedrock of the free enterprise system," who want to keep the door open to new business ventures, will have to do far more than voice the hope that it will happen. The problem has many complexities, but the actual experience in this valley deserves study in this connection.

I have discussed cases of conflicts, apparent or real, between the interests of private industry and the interest of the public, and how the TVA tries to bring those into a productive unity. Of course there are clashes which as of any given moment cannot be harmonized. The private interest must then be subordinated. But the area of conflicts that appear irreconcilable *can be reduced* to an extent not yet fully realized. Under modern conditions this will call for increased reliance upon the technician in industry and government rather than upon the "front man," including under technician, of course, the business manager and the administrator. And it is a job that can best be done close to the problem itself, where men are able to get beneath prejudices, dogmas, and broad generalizations, down to the facts themselves, the working facts.

It is here that TVA, working at the grass roots, has had such an advantage in its efforts, so largely successful, to eliminate or harmonize many conflicts which from a distance had always been assumed impossible of solution except by "fighting it out." For unless clashes of interest are examined on the spot, at the time they occur, by technicians who have a knack of getting at the facts and a deep desire to suggest practical alternatives, the conflict can soon become a deep issue, encrusted in prejudices, fed by ignorance or indifference to the facts, the subject of slogans and "crusades."

The experts, using the term in its broad, modern sense, have a central role to play not only in the development of harmony between private interests and the public interest, but in every facet of modern living. *The people and the experts:* the relation between them is of the greatest importance in the development of the new democracy. For the people are now helpless without the experts—the technicians and managers. This goes for all of us. Not only for the powerful industrial executive, the "big" investment banker, or the huge manufacturer of electric appliances, but for the farmer's wife, too, working in her poultry yard, the operator of a small planing mill in a remote town, the tobacco grower, the truck gardener and the dairyman, the coal mine operator, the little and big merchant, the county health official—wherever there are men engaged in growing or mining or transporting or processing or distributing goods, or maintaining government services.

One of the tasks of the administrator in public or private affairs who is committed to democratic principles is to devise ways of bringing modern science and technical skills to the hand of the layman. And this it is that TVA's work at the grass roots seeks to bring about. If the technical knowledge can be made to serve the individual in the daily decisions of his life, if it can be made to serve the common purpose of improving opportunity for human beings, that is an achievement of democracy in modern form and application.

This will require some drastic changes in the prevailing relations between experts and the people, both in industry and in government.

First of all, the experts and the people must be brought together. The technicians should live where the people they serve live. There are important exceptions, in highly specialized fields, but they do not affect the principle. An expert ought not to be remote from the problems the people face, and, although physical proximity will not guarantee closeness to the people, it will encourage it, whereas physical remoteness in distance definitely encourages, if it does not actually insure, remoteness in spirit and understanding, particularly in our country of vast area and great diversity in regional customs and natural conditions.

Keeping the experts and the people apart is not ordinarily due to the personal preference of the technical men. It is usually the result of a deliberate policy on the part of the executives, both in government and in private undertakings. When the technicians and the people live together, away from the central seat of power, by that very fact the power of knowledge and of decision is diffused. To some executives this in itself damns the idea, though the condemnation is usually wrapped in a jargon of administrative or business "principles."

The experts who live with the people should be the ablest men, not the weakest—not those left over after the needs of national conferences at headquarters in Washington or New York are cared for. The people's willingness to follow technical leadership—business and public alike—has already been impaired because so often the experts sent to the field from central headquarters are in responsibility little more than errand boys.

Bringing the technician physically face to face with the people's needs where they occur, in short, I regard as fundamental. This is what Congress made possible by setting up the TVA on a decentralized regional basis, a point I shall elaborate later.

Not only should the experts be brought to the people, but the different kinds of experts, working in special fields that are *related* in their effect upon the people, should live together and work together. Laymen cannot be expected to put together or understand the separate bits of a technical solution of their problems as they are worked out, separately, by specialized experts. And, unless specialists are required by appropriate managerial methods to live together and work together, they will not *unify their conclusions* so that they will make sense to the laymen who must put the results to use in their lives.

Technicians are more competent experts in their special fields when they live and work in the midst of lay problems. The education of the technician by the people themselves is only second in importance to the education of the laymen by the technician. Neither is possible at a distance in an atmosphere of remoteness, formal reports, memoranda, and the other trappings of absentee government and business.

Technicians will not be so likely to lose themselves in their work, hence will not be most effective, unless they can see that their talents are part of a whole task that appeals to them as important. Whether in private business or public service a man's conviction that he is performing an important service for others, that he is part of something far more important than himself, is a measure to him of the importance of that job. It is this, I think, that accounts in considerable part for the continued enthusiasm of the TVA technical staff long after the newness of the undertaking has passed, a spirit that has been observed and remarked upon by a long succession of visitors from other parts of the country and the world. The notion is naïve that only by the incentive of pay or profit do men "keep on their toes" and do their best work. Many of TVA's key staff members are earning less than in the posts they left to join this job.

People generally, I have found, place great importance upon

the development of resources for human well-being, especially if they are vividly made part of that effort. What they think of the importance of the expert's part in that job is mightily persuasive, to the expert, of the importance of his own task. And that to a considerable degree determines not only his personal satisfaction in it, but his effectiveness.

The experts who live with the people's problems are better able to learn of the people's aspirations, what it is that the people want and what they would want if they had available a knowledge of the alternatives from which they could make a choice. The people will not trust the experts and give them their confidence until they are persuaded that technicians in business as well as in government service are not setting up their own standards of what is "good for people." If technicians, by living with people, come to understand what the people want rather than what the experts want, then people will more and more repose confidence in them and their counsel, protect them from partisan and political attacks, and even help them further their specialized professional and scientific interests.

And the physical presence of the expert, the fact that he has elected to live with the people and their problems, to share their physical and social circumstances, will be accepted by laymen as one kind of proof of the sincere devotion of the expert to the improvement of the everyday living of the people, rather than to his own specialized interests and concerns. The technician, whether he be a forester, a social welfare worker, a manager, a financial or farm or mineral expert, has no more excuse to pursue his expertness simply for the pleasure its refinements give him or to increase his own or his profession's repute, than a physician at the bedside or a general in the field would be justified in following a particular course for comparable reasons of a personal or professional character.

Technicians must learn that explaining "why" to the people is generally as important (in the terms in which I am speaking) as "what" is done. To induce the action of laymen, which is the only way resource development is possible, "why" is almost always the key. Experts and managers at central business or government headquarters, isolated and remote, tend to become impatient of making explanations to the people. From impatience it is a short step to a feeling of superiority, and then to irresponsibility or dictation. And irresponsibility or dictation to the people, whether by experts or politicians or business managers or public administrators, is a denial of democracy.

Chapter 13

GOVERNMENT IN THE OPEN AIR

THE unified development of resources requires the broadest coalition of effort. This is a job not only for all the people, but for all of the people's institutions. The purpose is national, but the task is one that calls for a partnership of *every* agency of government, state and local as well as federal, that can further the common purpose. Therefore the grass-roots policy of drawing in private organizations and individuals—such as those of farmers, workers, and businessmen, discussed in preceding chapters—has in like manner been applied by TVA, a *federal* organization, so that the governmental agencies of *local* communities and of the *states* of the Tennessee Valley have become TVA's active and responsible partners.

Decentralizing the administration of government functions that are clearly national has been carried so far in this valley that it is literally true (I can think of no exceptions) that, whenever there is a state or a local institution which can perform part of the task that has been assigned by law to the TVA, we have sought to have that non-federal agency do it. This way of getting results is an exacting test of managerial skill in defining functions clearly and in securing a union of effort. Legalistic arguments about "states' rights" or "federal supremacy" have faded into irrelevance.

There is therefore nothing in this region's experience to support the genuine fears or the partisan outcry of ten years ago that setting up a federal regional agency would mean the undermining and ultimate destruction of state government and local communities. The contrary has been the case. It is indisputable from the record that state government is stronger in the Tennessee Valley today than it was ten years ago and has more functions to perform. It is notably true that local community government and functions are more vigorous. I know of no other place in the United States of which this can be said with equal basis in performance.

In developing extensive and close relations with state and local agencies TVA has not "discovered" a new principle. A number of other federal agencies have been making progress in this direction over a period of years. The TVA's demonstration of local-state-federal collaboration strengthens the hand of the many federal and state administrators and legislators who have been working to a similar purpose, against obstacles of indifference, hostility, and the inherent difficulties of the problem.

The device for effecting this widespread partnership relation with local and state government has been the written contract. There are now hundreds of such formal contracts between the TVA and every manner of public institution in the valley, ranging all the way from county library boards to state universities and the highway and conservation commissions.

These contracts are more than a definition of legal obligations. They constitute, too, expressed agreements on common purposes, often defined in broad terms. The discussions, arguments, and resolution of conflicting ideas and policies that precede final agreement serve a purpose almost as important, perhaps more important, than the contract itself. And as from time to time problems arise that are not covered by the contract (which, of course, is often the case) or if either agency is ready to add a new step in the relationship, a review of the broad purposes as well as the specific terms of the contract provides an occasion of great educational value. Instead of abstract talk about "cooperation" between local and federal agencies, the device of the contract encourages consideration of specific issues under existing conditions, but within the broad framework of the common purpose of strengthening the region. The bilateral contract, our experience has shown, is a device that lends itself to the needs of a relationship which to be most effective must recognize that it ought to be constantly changing and dynamic.

It is through such joint undertakings that many of the achievements I have pointed to as evidence of the great change have been accomplished. The scope of these partnership arrangements is broad and their content as richly varied as the valley's life itself: investigation of mica or manganese deposits; field tests of crop-bearing trees; development of a county recreational park for Negroes; work toward a specific cure for malaria; establishment of woodland wildlife refuges; forest-fire protection; housing; stream pollution and industrial water supply problems; preservation of archaeological materials; industrial research in flax processing; highway location; invention of a small dairy milk cooler, a trailer threshing machine, and many other similar farming devices—hundreds of joint enterprises, great and small. There are few agencies in these states of the Tennessee Valley that are not in this way a part of this national enterprise, as a result of deliberate policy.

Most of the activities thus carried on under these contracts by a community or state agency *could have been done by the TVA alone,* if the matter were viewed as a narrow issue of TVA's "prerogatives" or "jurisdiction." But dynamic decentralization is not concerned with the abstract issue of whether the national government under the Constitution has a superior "right" in a particular field from which it may exclude state and local action. TVA is charged with a broad national responsibility. Its function is that of leadership, stimulus, guidance: planning in the broadest sense.

In calling upon a state or local agency to share responsibility instead of setting up a TVA organization to do a specific job alone, and in negotiating the contracts upon which such joint efforts rest, we have deliberately tried to "start something" that local forces might later carry on, on their own. We have tried to place each new activity into the stream of the region's life, in the hands of local agencies to be continued when the initial

federal support is withdrawn. Grass-roots methods, decentralization as here applied, are therefore not simply the making of
"grants-in-aid" to state or local bodies, and the "matching of
federal funds" technique.

Let me take the growth of libraries as an example. The Authority wanted to provide library service for its thousands of employees building the Watts Bar Dam. But we did not want to
set up an independent library that would be closed and disappear once the dam was built. So TVA contracted with the
Tennessee Division of Libraries and the City Library Board of
Knoxville, to provide this service at an expense to us that did
not exceed what direct TVA library service would have cost.
These two agencies knew the people of the localities, knew
whom to turn to for local leadership. This contract then became
the nucleus for the development of local interest in library service, and regional library service grew naturally out of this beginning. As TVA construction work moved up the river to other
dams in counties near by, more and more local agencies and
leaders joined, all contributing funds raised by local town councils or county governments, until the library project had expanded into thirteen counties of east Tennessee, in only one of
which there had ever before been adequate public facilities for
the reading of books. Mobile library units were going through
the area, reaching TVA construction workers at their homes, and
also, under the terms of the contract, non-employees living in
the remote regions.

By the autumn of 1942 the Watts Bar Dam was nearly completed. TVA's contributions of funds would therefore soon be
terminated. Now came the real test of the methods we had in-
augurated. Had the roots sunk in deeply enough to sustain and
continue what was now under way? A meeting was called to see
what could be done to keep the regional library system operating. A dozen women and a half dozen men attended, representing the library boards of eleven out of thirteen of the counties,
and one by one they rose to tell of their experience. Mrs. Willis
Shadow of Meigs County began the discussion:

We have 6,000 people in Meigs County, and no railroad, no telephones, and no newspapers. The bookmobile and the grapevine are the only means of communication. If we lose the library bookmobile, how will we know what is going on in the world? What chance have we to improve standards of health or living except through reading? Talk about country people not reading! In Meigs County we read 4,000 books a month. There is not a family in the county that the library doesn't touch.

Many of these board members had been reluctant a year or two before to ask their county officers for a few hundred dollars' contribution to the regional library. Yet before the meeting adjourned they had all agreed to ask the State Legislature for an annual appropriation of $25,000. They organized a legislative committee and mobilized state-wide support. And on February 9, 1943, the Governor of Tennessee signed a measure setting up an east Tennessee regional library office, with an initial state appropriation of $20,000.

Three years had intervened between the beginning of the library program in the Watts Bar area and the state appropriation for the larger unit. In January, 1940, 263,000 people were practically destitute of books. Three years later these twelve counties, previously with none, now had 52,000 library books; the books were being distributed from two hundred locations covering the most remote limits of the area. Twenty-two thousand persons were registered as borrowers. In January, 1943, they read 250,000 books.

In these thirteen counties, the people, through their own efforts and with only indirect stimulation from TVA, have made a permanent advance in their level of living, and one of a nature which helps bring about other advances. The State Commissioner of Education, in a newspaper interview, expressed the opinion that the appropriation is the first step toward a statewide system of regional libraries, which may cost the state $250,000 "and will be worth every dollar of it." Already another group of Tennessee counties in another reservoir area, under a similar contract between TVA and state agencies, is planning to become a part of the state system two years hence.

This east Tennessee development is not unique. Up to the present time every library program for TVA employees that has been entrusted to local agencies for administration has grown into a permanent service when the Authority has withdrawn. Regional library systems covering three counties of northern Alabama and three counties of western North Carolina grew out of construction periods at the Guntersville and Hiwassee dams. It appears likely that out of these co-operative efforts between the TVA and institutions at the grass roots will come a complete coverage of the Tennessee Valley states with a useful and practical type of library organization.

In the same way and by similar devices the maintenance of public parks by local agencies has been expanded. Ten years ago, when the TVA began its work, there was little provision for outdoor public recreation in the whole valley. There was no state park system in Tennessee, no county had provided for park areas, neither Tennessee nor Alabama had a state department of conservation. Today both these states have active departments of conservation. There is the beginning of an excellent system of state and county parks, and plans are going forward for full utilization of the scenic and recreational resources of the region.

This began in 1934 when TVA developed several demonstration parks on land that lay on the margins of its reservoirs. Thousands of people in the valley visited these demonstration parks, approved the idea, and were ready to support efforts to further park developments. In this general public interest there was a basis either for expansion of TVA parks or of parks managed by state and local agencies. We chose the latter way.

In Tennessee TVA assisted in the drafting of state legislation creating a state Conservation Department. A state park system was begun. Continued under successive state administrations, and well supported at the state's sole expense, Tennessee now has one of the best state park systems in the Southeast. A comprehensive contract has been entered into between TVA and the State Department of Conservation, under which active collaboration is carried on in the development of scenic resources. TVA, as the owner of strips of land of great natural beauty bordering the new lakes, has leased a great deal of this land to the state and to county park commissions, at a nominal rental but under conditions that insure that the land will be used for public recreational uses and not inconsistently with the national functions for which it was originally purchased by TVA.

The TVA's program of industrial research in new methods of utilizing the valley's resources is a further illustration of the way agreements between the federal government and the states are used to advance this national program. Instead of our setting up entirely new facilities and personnel, this work, wherever possible, has been carried on in partnership with a state university engineering or agricultural research department. Time and again in a project initiated by the TVA or jointly by TVA and some state institution, TVA's financial and other contributions diminish or terminate while the state agency's increase or the project is taken over entirely. As a result of grass-roots methods the state's technical services are strengthened and stimulated, and at the same time TVA's national obligations are met, and at the lowest cost to the federal treasury.

For a federal agency to "work itself out of a job" in this way requires, among other things, that the state or local agency be given credit very generously for its part in these joint enterprises. Popular support depends upon it, and without that support, based upon wide understanding, local appropriations are difficult to secure, and inevitably dwindle and even disappear.

Realizing this, the TVA has been inclined to minimize its own role in initiating and stimulating such activities. Little has been known in the country at large of these activities. But there is danger to the entire program of regional resource development in this practice. TVA's policy of underscoring the role of its state partners and minimizing its own, could if carried to an extreme, prove to be self-defeating. The result would be lack of public support for TVA's own efforts. The state or local agency intended to be aided by TVA anonymity would instead be injured.

The farm problem illustrates the limitations on the method. It is almost incredible but nonetheless true that many farmers in the valley actually do not know that TVA has anything to do with the demonstration program initiated and financed by it. It is not unusual, for example, that in the office of a county agricultural agent administering the demonstration work the farmer will find bulletins and publicity about state and other federal agricultural agencies' work, but not a word about the TVA, though in that county the principal farm activity is area-wide demonstrations. By reason of its decision to work with existing state organizations TVA has failed to some extent to secure understanding and support for its land development program locally and through the country. The policies of some of the state agricultural agencies, for example, are by no means identical with those TVA itself might follow if we were carrying out the program by means of a separate TVA organization. But despite such occasional limitations I am certain that the method of working through state agencies has been entirely right, and that good results will be more enduring than if TVA had done the job through its own forces in a conventional way.

In this farm program the device of contracts with other existing agencies was followed from the very beginning, and has been carried out consistently through every step of the work. Written agreements providing for small-scale testing of TVA's new phosphatic fertilizer were first executed with the state agricultural experiment stations of the land-grant colleges of the valley. And, when the product was ready to be demonstrated in actual farming operations, the county agent was the man selected to assume general managerial responsibility for demonstration operations in the field, with the aid of an assistant to concentrate on demonstration supervision, the latter's compensation covered by TVA funds. The county agent is a local official, but he also represents and is partly compensated by the State Extension Service and the federal Department of Agriculture. An extensive Memorandum of Understanding was entered into between the TVA, the seven State Extension Services, and the Department of Agriculture, covering the new joint activities broadly and yet with considerable precision.

At the time this program was begun in 1934, many Tennessee Valley counties had failed to appropriate funds for their share of the county agent work, and so were without agents at all. A few months after the TVA program was under way, however, all but one of the counties in the valley had provided for full-time agents. In one county, for reasons of local politics, an appropriation for an agent was refused by the county government. A group of citizens raised the necessary funds by voluntary contributions so that the inauguration of the program need not be delayed until such time as the county politicians could be retired from office or induced to change their mind. A year later the county itself provided the funds. Today the number of state and local farm extension workers in the Tennessee Valley is the highest it has ever been; although the total central staff of TVA devoted to counsel and supervision of this joint enterprise work has never been large—thirty-eight in the beginning days of 1935—it is only fifty-three today.

Yet with this small federal staff a completely new program of soil rehabilitation and land use has been supervised; new concentrations and combinations of plant nutrients have revitalized the soil, new machinery and new techniques have raised the farmer's income; his self-interest and the nation's welfare have been joined. State and county institutions have been strengthened in the process. In this valley the muscles of local and state government are stronger. They are stronger because they are used.

The most far-reaching instance of a grass-roots partnership between local agencies and the TVA is afforded by the valley's power system. Now one of the largest power producers in the world, it presents the picture of a joint enterprise of the federal government and hundreds of local communities in six states, and the reliance for power of more than four million people. These communities range from small farming centers and mountain villages to a major city of a third of a million people.

Centralized large-scale production combined with decentralized, grass-roots local responsibility: this formula may prove of considerable importance in a number of other fields of business and of domestic and international governmental affairs.

Electricity, like the land, touches the everyday lives of people, directly and intimately. And yet the business of generating, transmitting, and distributing electricity is one of the most highly centralized industries in the United States. What TVA has done in decentralizing the service of this vital necessity of modern life may throw light not only upon public administration but also on how grass-roots methods may serve in a serious problem facing business generally.

Nowhere is the fear of bigness for bigness' sake and distrust of control from a far-off place better exemplified. People want not only government but also such essential services as electricity as close to them as possible.

A degree of centralization in a power system produces certain economies which cannot be effected in any other way. For some years I have been convinced, however, that a substantial measure of decentralized administration can be achieved with distinct social gains and without impairing the efficiency of the service. The power program of the Tennessee Valley constitutes the first large-scale demonstration by which the country can judge. Power generation and transmission require size and technical and physical integration to achieve economies. Here those responsibilities alone are centralized: the powerhouses and high-tension transmission network are operated directly by the TVA itself.

But the same principles of economy do not apply to the retail distribution of this "bulk electricity." And in the valley system the ownership and management of the *distribution* systems are decentralized. The decision to enter into a contract for wholesale power supply with TVA, and thereby to participate in the region-wide power program, was made voluntarily by each community, after public discussion, council meetings, referenda. Responsibility for those municipal and co-operative systems which deliver the power directly to the consumers who live in the cities, on the farms, and in the villages is lodged with the people themselves.

From the power plants on the river TVA is supplying power at wholesale to one hundred and twenty-nine separate and independent distribution systems, comprising hundreds of corporate or unincorporated communities. Forty-five of these systems are operated by co-operative associations. The remainder are operated by municipalities, several of which give county-wide service. *National* standards laid down by Congress in TVA's Act are maintained by means of provisions in the Authority's wholesale power contracts. In this way substantial uniformity of policy among its retail electricity distributors prevails in such important matters as rates, accounting, distribution of surplus revenues, and payments in lieu of taxes. But the ownership and control of the local electricity distribution systems are vested in the people themselves, usually through boards of trustees composed of local citizens. Within the area served by each of these one hundred and twenty-nine separate local agencies the citizens using electricity can place responsibility upon their own fellow citizens who represent them. If service within a city is inadequate, the local management is there close at hand and can readily be held accountable.

Each year a comparative financial and operating statement is issued, in which, in parallel columns, results are recorded for each of the one hundred and twenty-nine communities. If administrative costs per unit are higher in Community A than in Community B, the trustees in A can (and do) ask their superintendent for an explanation. If Community B piles up surpluses, reduces rates below the standard TVA rate, as a number of communities have done, that example is there before Community A and all the rest to emulate if they can. Since the accounts are all set up on a uniform basis, comparisons are readily made.

In a real sense the people in each community, therefore, within wide limits, themselves determine their own standards of efficiency of service and level of rates. They have an opportunity to learn at first hand the principles of public management and accountability, the evil consequences of allowing politics to enter into municipal services, the importance of putting electricity distribution in the hands of non-political boards made up largely of men with business experience. In contrast, the service departments of municipalities—water, streets, and the like—are in many communities headed by men whose previous experience is chiefly political. The comparison between the services rendered by the power boards and the other departments of the cities, in most instances, has been illuminating to the citizens.

In one Tennessee city the sentiment arising from this contrast was so marked that transfer to the power board of *all* the city's operating functions was actually proposed. In less drastic fashion, approval of these new standards of administration has led to the application of the public accounting practices that are now applied to electricity operations, to the non-electric operations of these communities.

The financial and operating results of this method of administering electricity supply have been good; many of them have been remarkable successes, with very high earnings and low unit operating costs. There is no occasion to go into the details here, but records are readily available as public documents.

The contagion of example has been active here as in almost every part of the changes in the region; and here again (as in the farm program) we have relied upon the benefits that come from learning by doing, rather than by "preaching" from on high, or by coercion. Bringing electricity back to the people in this way has tapped resources of local pride, ingenuity, and friendly rivalry with other communities which may mean as much to the Tennessee Valley a decade hence as the billions of kilowatt hours.

But the influence of this instance of decentralization goes beyond abundant and reliable electricity at low rates. For by this device a whole group of citizens and communities have taken themselves out of their strictly personal pursuits, to serve the interests of their neighbors and their whole community and region, with no other compensation, in most cases, than the prestige of leadership and the satisfaction of the task. As local power board members, they are in partnership with their national government, under a contract which for both locality and nation embodies a common purpose: the wide use of electricity for human welfare. They are not window-dressing to give a "local slant" to what is really a highly centralized undertaking, with the decisions actually made for them at remote headquarters. Disagreements occur from time to time between TVA and these local boards; and, though negotiations usually lead to agreement, it is quite a commonplace for a recommendation of TVA's staff, as originally proposed, to be rejected.

The responsibility for distribution supply, from the city gate to the electric refrigerator or the factory drill press, is solely theirs, subject only to broad policies that are part of a contract voluntarily entered into, which binds both the federal government and the local community. These boards are made up of men with every kind of background and interest: there are several bank presidents, a stockbroker, a labor leader, many farmers, lawyers, a druggist. They have an opportunity to take an active role in the entire development undertaking, of which this electricity operation in their town is a part. Not a few of the power boards have thus become a center of community initiative in industrial development, community planning, public recreation, post-war planning, and so on.

And thus still another group of the valley's citizens learn the lessons of the unity of resource development: the close interrelation between electricity and industry, between industry and farming, between farming and the building of the soil, between the soil and flood control. It will be seen that grass-roots democracy is throughout a story of the self-education of citizens. Men and women and children see their valley remade; they take part in that work. From this undertaking they have an opportunity to learn for themselves more of the basic lessons of nature and of human relations.

Chapter 14

DECENTRALIZATION: ANTIDOTE FOR
REMOTE CONTROL

But it is not wise to direct everything from Washington.
— PRESIDENT ROOSEVELT, Message to
the Congress respecting Regional
Authorities, June 3, 1937

WHAT I have been describing is the way by which in
this region we are working toward a decentralized administration of the functions of the central government.

The chief purpose of such methods of decentralization is to
provide greater opportunity for a richer, more interesting, and
more responsible life for the individual, and to increase his
genuine freedom, his sense of his own importance. Centralization in administration promotes remote and absentee control,
and thereby increasingly denies to the individual the opportunity
to make decisions and to carry those responsibilities by which
human personality is nourished and developed.

I find it impossible to comprehend how democracy can be a
living reality if people are remote from their government and in
their daily lives are not made a part of it, or if the control and
direction of making a living—industry, farming, the distribution
of goods—is far removed from the stream of life and from the
local community.

"Centralization" is no mere technical matter of "management,"
of "bigness versus smallness." We are dealing here with those
deep urgencies of the human spirit which are embodied in the
faith we call "democracy." It is precisely here that modern life
puts America to one of its most severe tests; it is here that the

experience in this valley laboratory in democratic methods takes on unusual meaning.

Congress established the TVA as a national agency, but one confined to a particular region. This provided an opportunity for decentralization. A limited region, its outlines drawn by its natural resources and the cohesion of its human interests, was the unit of federal activity rather than the whole nation.

To the degree that the experiment as administered helps to solve some of the problems raised by the flight of power to the center and the isolation of the citizen from his government, history may mark that down as TVA's most substantial contribution to national well-being and the strengthening of democracy.

TVA's methods are, of course, not the only ones that must be tried. There will be different types and other methods of administration suitable to other problems and different areas. Diversity will always be the mark of decentralized administration, just as surely as uniformity (often for its own sake) is the mark of central and remote control.

Decentralization in action has been anything but an easy task. Its course will never be a smooth one, without setbacks and disappointments. Everywhere, nevertheless, the problem must be faced if we are to conserve and develop the energies and zeal of our citizens, to keep open the channels through which our democracy is constantly invigorated.

Overcentralization is, of course, no unique characteristic of our own national government. It is the tendency all over the world, in business as well as government. Centralization of power at our national capital is largely the result of efforts to protect citizens from the evils of overcentralization in the industrial and commercial life of the country, a tendency that has been going on for generations. Chain stores have supplanted the corner grocery and the village drug store. In banks and theaters, hotels, and systems of power supply—in every activity of business —local controls have almost disappeared. To be sure, business centralization has brought advantages in lower unit costs and improved services. Except by the village dressmaker, or the owner of the country store or hotel, the advantages of centralization, at the beginning, at least, were gratefully received. People seemed to like a kind of sense of security that came with uniformity.

The paying of the price came later when towns and villages began to take stock. The profits of local commerce had been siphoned off, local enterprise was stifled, and moribund communities awoke to some of the ultimate penalties of remote control. When a major depression struck in 1929, business centralization made us more vulnerable than ever before to the disruption that ensued. Power had gone to the center, decisions were made far from the people whose lives would be affected. Cities and states were powerless to meet the evils that were bred; the federal government had to act. The tendency to centralization in government was quickened.

It was ironic that centralized businesses should become, as they did, eloquent advocates of the merits of decentralization in government. From their central headquarters they began to issue statements and brochures. And a wondrous state of confusion arose in the minds of men: they ate food bought at a store that had its replica in almost every town from coast to coast; they took their ease in standard chairs; they wore suits of identical weave and pattern and shoes identical with those worn all over the country. In the midst of this uniformity they all listened on the radio to the same program at the same time, a program that bewailed the evils of "regimentation," or they read an indignant editorial in their local evening papers (identical with an editorial that same day in a dozen other newspapers of the same chain) urging them to vote for a candidate who said he would bring an end to centralization in government.

I am not one who is attracted by that appealing combination of big business and little government. I believe that the federal government must have large grants of power progressively to deal with problems that are national in their consequences and remedy, problems too broad to be handled by local political units. I am convinced, as surely most realistic men must be, that in the future further responsibilities will have to be assumed by the central government to deal with national issues which centralized business inevitably creates. The war has advanced this trend.

The people have a right to demand that their federal government provide them an opportunity to share in the benefits of advances in science and research, the right to demand protection from economic abuses beyond the power of their local political units to control. But they have the further right to insist that the methods of administration used to carry out the very laws enacted for their individual welfare will not atrophy the human resources of their democracy.

It is folly to forget that the same dangers and the same temptations exist whether the centralization is in government or in mammoth business enterprises. In both cases the problem is to capture the advantages that come with such centralized authority as we find we must have, and at the same time to avoid the hazards of overcentralized *administration* of those central powers.

It can be done. It can be done in many business operations as well as in government activities. I have described the way in which the operations of the Tennessee Valley's power system have been brought close to the people of this valley. Certainly that makes clear that no blind fear of bigness underlies my conviction of the necessity for decentralized administration. Here we have centralized only the activities in connection with electric supply which are common to a large integrated area and can best be carried on by a single agency, that is, producing the power and then transmitting it from the dams and steam-electric plants to the gates of communities. But, as I have pointed out, in the Tennessee Valley system the ownership and management of the distribution systems are decentralized. Here, I believe, is one example, among many, of an effective combination of the advantages of the *decentralized administration of centralized authority*.

The distinction between authority and its administration is

a vital one. For a long time all of us—administrators, citizens, and politicians—have been confused on this point. We have acted on the assumption that because there was an increasing need for centralized authority, the centralized execution of that authority was likewise inevitable. We have assumed that, as new powers were granted to the government with its seat at Washington, these powers therefore must also be administered from Washington. Out of lethargy and confusion we have taken it for granted that the price of federal action was a top-heavy, cumbersome administration. Clearly this is nonsense. *The problem is to divorce the two ideas of authority and administration of authority.*

Our task is to invent devices of management through which many of the powers of the central government will be administered not by remote control from Washington but in the field.

A national capital almost anywhere is bound to suffer from lack of knowledge of local conditions, of parochial customs. And in a country as vast as the United States, in which local and regional differences are so vital and so precious, many citizens and administrators are coming to see more and more that powers centrally administered from Washington cannot take into account the physical and economic variations within our boundaries. The national strength and culture that flows from that very diversity cannot be nourished by centralized administration.

It has become common observation that in Washington it is too easy to forget, let us say, the centuries of tradition that lie behind the customs of the Spanish-American citizens in New Mexico and how different their problems are from those of the men and women whose lives have been spent in the mountains of the South. It is hard, from a distance, with only memoranda before him, for an administrator to be alive to the fact that the ways of suburban New Jersey are alien to the customs of the coast of eastern Maine. And yet the fact that the ancestors of these people brought dissimilar customs from their homelands, that they have earned their living in different manners, that the climates in which they live are not the same—this is all deeply important when a national program is brought to the men and women in cities and villages and farms for application, when their daily lives are visibly affected. When those differences in customs are not comprehended, statutes seem irrelevant or harsh. They destroy confidence, and disturb rather than promote people's welfare.

Centralization at the national capital or within a business undertaking always glorifies the importance of pieces of paper. This dims the sense of reality. As men and organizations acquire a preoccupation with papers they become less understanding, less perceptive of the reality of those matters with which they should be dealing: particular human problems, particular human beings, actual things in a real America—highways, wheat, barges, drought, floods, backyards, blast furnaces. The reason why there is and always has been so much bureaucratic spirit, such organizational intrigue, so much pathologic personal ambition, so many burning jealousies and vendettas in a capital city (any capital city, not only Washington), is no mystery. The facts with which a highly centralized institution deals tend to be the men and women of that institution itself, and their ideas and ambitions. To maintain perspective and human understanding in the atmosphere of centralization is a task that many able and conscientious people have found well-nigh impossible.

Making decisions from papers has a dehumanizing effect. Much of man's inhumanity to man is explained by it. Almost all great observers of mankind have noted it. In *War and Peace* Tolstoy makes it particularly clear. Pierre Bezukhov is standing a captive before one of Napoleon's generals, Marshal Davout.

At the first glance, when Davout had only raised his head from *the papers where human affairs and lives were indicated by numbers*, Pierre was merely a circumstance, and Davout could have shot him without burdening his conscience with an evil deed, but now he saw in him a human being . . .

To see each citizen thus as a "human being" is easy at the grass roots. That is where more of the functions of our federal government should be exercised.

The permanence of democracy indeed demands this. For the cumulative effect of overcentralization of administration in a national capital is greatly to reduce the effectiveness of government. It is serious enough in itself when, because of remoteness and ignorance of local conditions or the slowness of their operation, laws and programs fail of their purposes. We are threatened, however, with an even more disastrous sequence, the loss of the people's confidence, the very foundation of democratic government. Confidence does not flourish in a "government continually at a distance and out of sight," to use the language of Alexander Hamilton, himself a constant advocate of strong central authority. On the other hand, said Hamilton,

the more the operations of the national authority are intermingled in the ordinary exercise of government, the more the citizens are accustomed to meet with it in the common occurrences of their political life, the more it is familiarized to their sight and to their feelings, the further it enters into those objects which touch the most sensible chords and put into motion the most active springs of the human heart, the greater will be the probability that it will conciliate the respect and attachment of the community.

When "the respect and attachment of the community" give place to uneasiness, fears develop that the granting of further powers may be abused. Ridicule of the capriciousness of some government officials takes the place of pride. Democracy cannot thrive long in an atmosphere of scorn or fear. One of two things ultimately happens: either distrustful citizens, their fears often capitalized upon by selfish men, refuse to yield to the national government the powers which it should have in the common interest; or an arrogant central government imposes its will by force. In either case the substance of democracy has perished.

We face a dilemma; there is no reason to conceal its proportions. I do not minimize the complexities and difficulties it presents. We need a strong central government. This is plain to everyone who sees the changed nature of our modern world. But I have deep apprehension for the future unless we learn how many of those central powers can be decentralized in their administration.

Every important administrative decision need not be made in Washington. We must rid ourselves of the notion that a new staff, with every member paid out of the federal treasury, has to administer every detail of each new federal law or regulation. We who believe devoutly in the democratic process should be the first to urge the use of methods that will keep the administration of national functions from becoming so concentrated at the national capital, so distant from the everyday life of ordinary people, as to wither and deaden the average citizen's sense of participation and partnership in government affairs. *For in this citizen participation lies the vitality of a democracy.*

Federal functions can be decentralized in their administration. But it requires a completely changed point of view on the part of citizens and their representatives. For this business of centralization is not wholly the fault of government administrators. Statutes are rarely designed to provide an opportunity for ingenuity in the development of new techniques in administration. Only infrequently do you find a new law which in its terms recognizes the hazards of overcentralization.

Our recent history shows that many public men and editorial writers prefer the privilege of berating administrators as "bureaucrats" to suggesting and supporting ways through which the vices of bureaucracy would have less opportunity to develop. Congress has usually taken the easy course, when new laws are passed, of piling upon the shoulders of an already weary (but rarely unwilling) official the responsibility for supervising a whole new field of federal activity. He has been given a fresh corps of assistants perhaps, but upon his judgment decisions of great detail ultimately rest.

This country is too big for such a pyramiding of responsibilities. In the general atmosphere of bigness, men continue to come about the same size. There is a limit to the energy and wisdom of the best; the ancient lust for power for its own sake burns in the worst.

In the case of TVA, Congress did enact a statute which permitted a decentralized administration. Had not Congress created that opportunity, the TVA could not have developed its administration at the grass roots. An area of manageable proportions—the watershed of a river as its base—was the unit of administration. Decisions could be made and responsibility taken at a point that was close to the problems themselves. That is the test of decentralization.

It is not decentralization to open regional offices or branches in each state, if decisions have to be made in Washington and the officers in the field prove to be merely errand boys. Genuine decentralization means an entirely different point of view in the selecting and training of personnel. It means an emigration of talent to the grass roots. But if the important tasks, the real responsibilities, are kept at the center, men of stature will not go to the "field."

Neither is it decentralization when bureaus or departments are moved out of crowded Washington. It may be necessary and entirely wise—but it is not decentralization. You do not get decentralization as we know it in the TVA unless you meet two tests:

First, do the men in the field have the power of decision?

Second, are the people, their private and their local public institutions, actively participating in the enterprise?

There is generous lip service to decentralization on every hand. But little will be done about it unless there is real understanding of what it means, and an urgent and never ceasing demand from citizens.

When methods such as those the TVA has used are proposed, the chief objection usually made is that local communities, state agencies, or the field officers of federal agencies cannot be trusted to carry out national policies. Usually the reason is dressed up in more tactful language, but, however disguised, it is the doctrine of the elite nevertheless. The burden of proving that the men who at the time are federal officials in Washington are the only ones competent to administer the laws enacted by

Congress certainly lies upon those who advance that reason. Actually such statements often prove the desperate hazards of centralization to the health of a democracy, for they exhibit, in the minds of those who put them forward, a low esteem or affectionate contempt for the abilities of anyone outside the capital city, or else a slavish concern for the existing rituals of bureaucracy.

There are of course many instances where the facts appear to support the claim that good administration of national concerns cannot be obtained through the co-operation of local agencies. Local politics, ineptitude, lack of interest and experience in public matters and in administration, brazen partisanship, even corruption—all these stand in the way. I am sure these hazards exist. I am sure, for we have encountered most of them in this valley. But what are the alternatives? Fewer citizens participating in governmental administration. Less and less local community responsibility. More federal employees in the field armed with papers to be filled out and sent to Washington for "processing," because only there is "good administration" possible. The progressive atrophy of citizen interest. An ever wider gulf between local communities and national government, between citizens and their vital public concerns. Such are the alternatives.

The often flabby muscles of community and individual responsibility will never be invigorated unless the muscles are given work to do. They grow strong by use; there is no other way. Although it is true that decentralization at times is ineffective because of the quality of local officials or field officers, the virtues, by comparison, of what can be done in central headquarters are somewhat illusory. For, without the co-operation of citizens (an admittedly difficult goal) and of institutions familiar to them, no detailed and far-reaching economic or social policy and no democratic planning can be made effective. Surely there can be little doubt about the truth of this statement, as I write these words, in our second year at war. The daily experience of the average citizen confirms it unanswerably.

The shortcomings of highly centralized administration of national policies are not due simply to the stupidity or wrongheadedness of particular individuals. Naming a scapegoat whenever a mess is uncovered, a favorite editorial and lay custom, is of little help; it usually misses the mark. We need perspective about such things, lest we foolishly take out our anger and frustration for ineptitudes upon this man and that, this party or that, instead of turning our attention where it usually belongs, *viz.*, upon the limitations and dangers of centralization.

These evils are inherent in the overcentralized administration of huge enterprise, because it ignores the nature of man. There is light on this matter in the words of de Tocqueville, writing a century ago of the relatively simple society of the United States.

However enlightened and however skillful a central power may be [he wrote in his *Democracy in America*] it cannot of itself embrace all the details of the existence of a great nation. . . . And when it attempts to create and set in motion so many complicated springs, it must submit to a very imperfect result, or consume itself in bootless efforts. Centralization succeeds more easily, indeed, in subjecting the external actions of men to a certain uniformity . . . and perpetuates a drowsy precision in the conduct of affairs, which is hailed by the heads of the administration as a sign of perfect order . . . in short, it excels more in prevention than in action. Its force deserts it when society is to be disturbed or accelerated in its course; and if once the co-operation of private citizens is necessary to the furtherance of its measures, the secret of its impotence is disclosed. Even while it invokes their assistance, it is on the condition that they shall act exactly as much as the government chooses, and exactly in the manner it appoints. . . . These, however, are not conditions on which the alliance of the human will is to be obtained; its carriage must be free, and its actions responsible, or such is the constitution of man the citizen had rather remain a passive spectator than a dependent actor in schemes with which he is unacquainted.

Out of my experience in this valley I am as acutely aware as anyone could be of the difficulties of securing the active participation of citizens at the grass roots. I know "what a task" (again using the words of de Tocqueville) it is "to persuade men to busy themselves about their own affairs." But our experience here has in it more of encouragement than of despair. For in this valley, in almost every village and town and city, in every rural community, there has proved to be a rich reservoir of citizen talent for public service. The notion that brains, resourcefulness, and capacity for management are a limited commodity in America—and this it is that is behind most of the skepticism about decentralization—is a myth that is disproved in almost every chapter and page of the story of the development of this valley.

The fact that TVA was not remote but close at hand has been the most effective way to dissipate the considerable initial suspicion of this enterprise and secure from citizens of every point of view the existing wide measure of warm co-operation. In the case of the power program of the TVA, for example, if TVA were not in the region and of it, if it could not make decisions until Washington, hundreds of miles away, had "processed" the papers and reached a conclusion, only a few of these valley communities, in my opinion, would have signed a contract with the TVA for power supply. Remote control from Washington would not have seemed greatly to be preferred to remote control from a holding company office in New York. And if TVA had not in turn decentralized its own operations the plan would work badly. TVA's division and area managers and other field officials are not merely office boys with imposing titles but no standing or authority. They are selected, trained, given broad responsibility and discretion, and compensated accordingly.

The decentralized administration of federal functions is no infallible panacea. Of course mistakes are made at the grass roots too. But even the mistakes are useful, for they are close at hand where the reasons behind them can be seen and understood. The wise decisions, the successes (and there are many such), are a source of pride and satisfaction to the whole community. If, as I strongly believe, power must be diffused, if it is vital that citizens participate in the programs of their government, if it is important that confidence in our federal government be maintained, then decentralization is essential.

I speak of decentralization as a problem for the United States of America. But the poison of overcentralization is not a threat to us here alone. Decentralized administration is one form of antidote that is effective the world over, for it rests upon human impulses that are universal. Centralization is a threat to the human spirit everywhere, and its control is a concern of all men who love freedom.

Chapter 15

REGIONAL PILLARS OF DECENTRALIZATION

I hope this will be an age of experiments in government.
—THOMAS JEFFERSON

YOU cannot, of course decentralize the functions of the federal government if the whole nation is the operating unit for the carrying out of national powers. Obviously some smaller area than the whole country must be used. In the case of the TVA, Congress and the President determined that in the development of resources that smaller unit should be based upon the natural region; this region is described in the language of the 1933 enactment as "the Tennessee River drainage basin and . . . such adjoining territory as may be related to or materially affected by the development consequent to this Act. . . ."

The use of the region as an autonomous unit of development was a deliberate "experiment." The results of this departure in national policy were to be reported to the nation and become the object of study as to its effectiveness. It was anticipated at the time that if the experiment commended itself by its results the method might be followed or adapted to other regions. The idea that the Tennessee Valley region was set up as a kind of testing ground for the nation has been often expressed, and appears in the President's original message: "If we are successful here," he said, "we can march on, step by step, in a like development of other great natural territorial units within our borders."

The application of TVA's results in decentralized regional development to other parts of the country has become a question of some practical consequence, since from time to time bills providing for regional developments have been introduced in Congress. These proposals, some now pending, are often described or are promoted as measures that provide a "TVA" for this or that area of the country.

That the letters TVA should be thus used as a kind of symbol for resource development is pleasing to us, naturally. But references to TVA in connection with such proposals are inaccurate and misleading unless they do in fact adopt the TVA idea in its essentials,

—a federal autonomous agency, with authority to make its decisions in the region

—responsibility to deal with resources, as a unified whole, clearly fixed in the regional agency, not divided among several centralized federal agencies

—a policy, fixed by law, that the federal regional agency work co-operatively with and through local and state agencies.

The entire TVA experiment, as I interpret it, makes it clear that no proposal for regional resource development may be described as a kind of "TVA" unless it embodies these fundamentals, which are clearly written into the TVA Act and have been the very heart and spirit of ten years of transforming that law into action.

My concern here is not whether in future legislation Congress decides to follow or to abandon these principles embodied in the TVA; this book has a deeper purpose than merely to serve as a polemic urging more regional authorities along TVA principles. But I have a responsibility to point out that, in the discussions of future resource policy, merely adopting the nomenclature "regional authority" or "regional administration" is not in itself an adoption of the TVA idea.

What constitutes a region? How large should it be for most effective development? I have no confidence in the elaborate rituals by which some technicians think they can determine what constitutes a region. No one can work out a formula for what is in reality a judgment that does not lend itself to such precise measurement. On this issue of what constitutes a region and upon the general philosophy of regionalism there is a substantial literature to which those who wish to pursue the subject are referred.

There is, however, one generalization which our specific experience in the TVA does support: the regions should not be so large that they are not, in a management sense, of "workable" size. The full potentialities of the unified approach to resources, and the opportunity to be close to the people and their problems, may be fatally impaired if the region itself is a vast one.

In my judgment the present TVA region ought not to be substantially enlarged. This "region"—the watershed plus the area of electric service that extends outside the drainage basin substantially as that area is now constituted—is about as large as it ever should be. The proposal now pending in Congress (once approved by the Senate) to add to the TVA's responsibility the development of the Cumberland River will probably be adopted after the war. This is sound. That river lies within the region and adjoins the drainage line, emptying into the Ohio two or three miles from the mouth of the Tennessee. The people of the Cumberland Valley are already participating in parts of the enterprise, and they understand it. But, with that exception and some extension of electricity beyond the area presently served, I feel strongly that substantial additions to the territorial scope of the TVA would impair its effectiveness and threaten the onset of the evils of remoteness we seek to remedy.

Those who come to have confidence in the TVA idea and seek to have it put into effect in their own regions should be warned that the task is one of adaptation and not of copying or imitation. Indeed, it is the strength of the regional idea that it tends to nourish regional differences in traditions, culture, and ways of living, without sacrifice of national unity on other fundamentals. National unity, but unity through diversity, is the essential meaning of the nation's motto, *E Pluribus Unum*.

I would be rendering a disservice if I left the impression that the TVA's methods offer a ready-made pattern to be copied literally, in all manner of situations, or that genuine decentralization in the administration of every and any kind of national function is feasible. Many functions of the federal government present entirely different problems from the development and improvement of land, water, forests, minerals. Resources have a fixed *situs* and can only be dealt with adequately at that *situs*. TVA's methods can be readily adapted to such problems. But whether regional decentralization in the genuine sense is feasible for many other functions is not a subject for generalization. While different devices must be invented, TVA's methods and experience may be of considerable aid in that process.

All through the public service and in business able men are concerning themselves with such inventions, often with notable results. The practices of decentralized administration have made considerable headway; the tendency, however, continues the other way. Lip service is paid to decentralization by legislators and administrators; they then proceed to draw to Washington the very elements of discretion and the power to decide which impose centralization in its worst forms. Members of Congress will inveigh against the evils of "concentrating power in Washington," and then almost in the same breath (unwittingly, without a doubt) will speed up that very process by passing legislation that sets up additional managerial controls in a central Washington bureau. An able Member of Congress, sincerely interested in the necessity of federal decentralization, recently introduced a comprehensive resolution proposing a broad study of the means of achieving decentralization in the government; but only a few months later the same Member introduced another measure to combine all federally owned power operations in a central "power administration" in Washington!

The issue of regional decentralization is further clouded by simple naïveté. The mere moving of personnel out of Washington to some other city as a result of wartime congestion is regarded by many as "decentralization." This may simply be a rather expensive form of centralization. And then there is a tendency to obscure the issue and distract attention from the heart of the problem by arguments about quite irrelevant or relatively unimportant details. Thus there is sometimes a great to-do about whether a regional agency should be headed by a board of three members or by a single administrator. This of course has nothing whatever to do with the region as a unit of decentralization.

There is another and more subtle way of avoiding the real issue in regionalism: to paint a glowing detailed picture of the opportunities for regional development and the virtues of regionalism, and then to fail to discuss *how* these happy results are to be secured. This blandly ignores the fact that the particularized benefits so persuasively portrayed have, as a matter of historical fact, never been achieved by any of the traditional methods of resource development. If this manner of presentation does not show lack of candor it displays a failure to understand the essential relation that means bear to results. The public is entitled to a realistic and candid discussion of precisely what is involved in regional decentralization. If a particular goal is described specifically, the method for reaching it should be disclosed with equal particularity; it cannot be ignored as an "administrative detail."

There are some opponents of decentralization and regionalism who face the issue squarely. I shall not, of course, attempt to state or to answer any but the principal of their objections, some of which are put in the highly technical jargon of expertise. Behind the multiplicity of words there is often concealed some bureau's or department's "vested right" in centralized government. In this the public is little interested. It does not interest me either, for I fail to see the relevance of such an objection.

The objection that regionalism will "Balkanize" the country is a familiar and candid one usually sincerely raised. The argument is that regionalism is a kind of provincialism that divides rather than unites the country, underlining sectional animosities and obstructing a really national outlook. But such a position shows a lack of understanding of our history and of the nature of regionalism. It assumes first of all that regions, rather than the individual states, have not always been the units of important national policy development, as scholars such as Turner have made clear and as public men understand so well. In the Congressional Record we read of "the Gentleman from Indiana" or New York or Texas. The newspapers however are more realistic. They report the plans, meetings, and votes of the "Senators from the Corn Belt," or the "cotton bloc," or the "New England delegation in Congress."

For the practical purposes of federal legislation, this is a country of regions, not states.

The growth and development of our national policies is not the result of conflicts between states; it represents an attempted reconciliation between the interests of the various natural regions. Debates on such subjects as the tariff, inland waterway improvements, or measures relating to agriculture almost always foreshadowed votes cast for the most part on a sectional basis. It was not a war between separate states which settled one great economic and political conflict in this country. It was strife between sections. And, although only once in its history has this country resorted to arms to settle regional differences, our national policies have always been arrived at through compromises—often very costly ones to the nation's interest—between the points of view of different sections of the country. Each region has fought for its own interests, usually with little regard to the effect on the country as a whole. This is sectionalism. We avoid the word today, hoping perhaps that the evils of disunity and local selfishness will vanish if the syllables are forgotten. But it is not so easily exorcised.

• Modern regionalism, by contrast, rests squarely upon the supremacy of the *national* interest. It admits that there are problems and resources common to areas larger than any single state—a river basin, for example. It recognizes that certain points of view develop in some portions of the country and are not shared by the nation as a whole. It affirms and insists, however, that the solution of regional problems and the development of regional resources are *matters of concern to the whole country*. It proposes to harmonize regional advancement with the national welfare. That concern for and supremacy of the national interest distinguishes "regionalism" from "sectionalism." Under the banner of sectionalism, states throughout our history have combined to support or to oppose federal action. Under the modern concept of regionalism, the federal government acts to meet regional needs to the end that the entire nation may profit.

The organization of the Tennessee Valley Authority is an example of this modern idea of regionalism. To create it seven states did not unite to demand special privileges to distinguish them from the country as a whole, regardless of the ensuing consequences to the national welfare. The federal legislature itself created an independent regional agency whose basic objective was to conserve the natural resources lying in the valley of the Tennessee and to develop those resources *in conformity with broad national objectives and policies*. This is the very opposite—indeed it is the antidote—of "Balkanization."

The idea of regionalism embodied in the TVA—a federal agency decentralized in fact—offers a rational way of harmonizing regional interests with the national interest. For the first time a federal implement is at hand for that task, to take the place of the usual method of political bargaining, so often wholly crude and without a basis in facts, policy, or principle.

An interesting illustration of how TVA functions in this balancing of regional and national concerns is afforded by the process by which the TVA Act was amended in 1940, to increase the payments in lieu of taxes on TVA's property which it is authorized to make to local and state agencies of the valley. The issue presented a sharp conflict between regional and national interests. Since, of course, federal property may not be taxed by the states, the Tennessee Valley region wanted Congress to consent to the largest possible tax payments from the federal government's TVA. The national government's interest, on the other hand, was in having returned to its treasury the maximum amount of TVA's surplus power revenues, and that meant consent to only a minimum tax payment to the valley. An analogous conflict has been before the national Congress on many occasions. In one case the bitter controversy reached a climax when Oklahoma's Governor called out state troops, the state by this show of force displaying its dissent to federal policy.

But in adjusting this kind of region-nation conflict in the Tennessee Valley, for the first time Congress could determine the issue on a record of facts and with a consideration of principle. For it was TVA's duty to prepare itself to make a balanced presentation. Hence consideration of the problem was not on the level of a mere show of voting strength, or log-rolling, or some haphazard and casual solution. To be successful in the discharge of this function it was necessary that TVA have the confidence of the region, and yet prove to Congress that it was putting national interests first.

TVA made an exhaustive analysis of the facts respecting local tax problems as a result of TVA property purchases, the prospects for the future, the benefits received by the region from federal funds. The details of the varying tax laws of several different states were analyzed closely. Then TVA representatives conferred with the governors and fiscal officers of all the states, of many counties with peculiarly difficult problems, with tax consultants, and with federal tax officials. As a result a measure was drafted which embodied principles that TVA as a national agency could recommend. And, although far short of the original claims of local tax bodies, its fairness led all the states to concur. After exhaustive Congressional committee hearings, the bill as recommended by the TVA and agreed to by the states was passed. Under this law TVA has paid, to the end of the fiscal year 1943, out of its power revenues, a total of $5,320,000 in tax payments to states and counties of the valley; in the single fiscal year ended June 30, 1943, the total of these payments was about two million dollars.

There are many other instances of the way a federal regional agency, though understanding and sympathizing with regional concerns, can *further the national interest in a cohesion of all regions*; this is in contrast with the evils of sectionalism, for it adds to national strength. Early in its history, for example, the TVA took a firm stand against any policy of inducing existing industry located in other regions to move to the Tennessee Valley. Important as industrial development in this region seemed, it was clear that our national obligation would be violated by such a practice of pirating industry. It is significant that this policy, initially viewed here with disapproval, now has nearly universal support from the valley itself, long become accustomed to such raiding practices by some private agencies. The practices of inducing industry to change location by offering tax exemptions, free land and buildings, and the lure of "cheap and docile labor," practices that stir up interregional animosities and distrust, are today definitely under a cloud of disapproval by the business interests of this valley.

In quite a different way the TVA, by relating the interests of this region to the national interest, has been able to promote national strength. An illustration is afforded by the development of a blast furnace to convert the phosphate ores of the Far West into fertilizer materials. The starting point was, of course, the need of the Tennessee Valley region. The high-grade phosphate ores of Tennessee are too limited in extent to continue to support the land needs of so large a part of the United States as they are being called upon to serve. In the Far West on the public domain there existed almost limitless supplies. The TVA electric furnace, newly designed, would have been ideal for the processing of these far western deposits for use as fertilizer on farms of the Middle West. The electric furnace, however, was not practical for these western ores, because essential low-cost electric power was not near enough at hand. A new blast furnace, which could use readily available western fuels, was the TVA chemical engineers' answer. The *national* interest in building the land of the Midwest was furthered by a *regional* interest in preventing the premature exhaustion of the mineral resources of the Southeast.

It is worth while to contrast the performance of a regional national agency under such circumstances with the unhappy record of state embargoes and other trade barriers that have been resorted to in the past, in a local or sectional spirit, in analogous and sometimes parallel situations.

Regionalism can try out and demonstrate on a limited scale methods of development and of administration that are then open to use for the whole nation. The origin of the TVA itself illustrates the point. Franklin D. Roosevelt in New York State and George W. Norris in Nebraska saw the importance and value of regional planning of resources. They urged the setting up of a national experiment, in a southern region, which would be available for appraisal by every region. Experimentation and demonstration of the value of complete river planning, reliance upon reservoirs for flood control, multiple-purpose dams instead of limited-purpose structures—once these have been tried out on a drainage-basin scale in this valley region, they can and are being applied elsewhere. Similarly with new methods of administration: some of the specific steps toward regional decentralization, among other federal agencies, are directly attributable to public knowledge and approval of the successful experience in this one valley.

Regionalism is strengthening, not dividing, the nation. TVA was launched in such a setting of national interest; as President-elect Roosevelt said in January, 1933, in an informal speech in the South, it was

more today than a mere opportunity for the Federal Government to do a kind turn for the people in one small section of a couple of States . . . [It was an] opportunity to accomplish a great purpose for the people of many States and, indeed, for the whole Union. Because there we have an opportunity of setting an example of planning, not just for ourselves but for the generations to come, tying in industry and agriculture and forestry and flood prevention, tying them all into a unified whole over a distance of a thousand miles so that we can afford better opportunities and better places for living for millions of yet unborn in the days to come.

In many matters of detail the TVA demonstrates the contrast between selfish sectionalism and national regionalism. TVA's personnel by a deliberate policy is selected from every part of the United States, whereas a narrow, sectional interest would follow the provincial practice in many cities and states of confining public employment to local citizens. The way in which the TVA has "loaned" its technical personnel to many other government agencies points in the same direction; the Bonneville Administration in the Northwest, the Santee-Cooper development in South Carolina, the Colorado River Authority in Texas are examples. In one degree or another these and other agencies have shared the lessons of the Tennessee Valley's experience and methods, even in such details of management as land purchasing, electric rate schedules, personnel management, accounting. Because the TVA has thus been called upon for aid in problems in other parts of the country (and more recently in foreign countries) the danger that this regional agency might fall into a narrow provincialism, the very antithesis of a national outlook, has been kept to a minimum.

"If there were a number of regional authorities like the TVA how could they possibly be co-ordinated?" This question is usually asked as if there could be but one answer, and that one a complete refutation of regionalism. It is sometimes coupled with the assertion, intended to show friendliness to the regional idea: "TVA has proved to be effective; but that is because there is only one TVA."

These critics offer the spectacle of a nation in which regional authorities would each be going its separate way, resulting in chaos or requiring elaborate administrative "co-ordination" in Washington. These fears call for some comment, based upon TVA's experience.

Surely it is not fear of conflicts on *policy* on which these concerns center. The policies that a regional authority must pursue are, of course, national policies. The broad structure of these policies must be determined by Congress. It is, of course, the highest function of Congress and the President to resolve just such conflicts in policy affecting the whole nation. The regional authority provides an instrument for assisting in reasoned settlement of such differing policies. Provided the legislation creating the regional pillars of decentralization is so drawn that Congress passes upon and defines fundamental policies, there would seem to be little basis for fears in this direction.

If not policy co-ordination, just what, then, is the nature of these apprehensions of conflicts between regional authorities, this fear of "lack of co-ordination"? The real issue is not lack of co-ordination in policies, but the fact that the decentralized administration of federal functions will not result in *operating uniformity*. The actual concern is that in one region problems will be administered in a different way from what they are in another.

It is important to examine this apprehension. And it clarifies the nature of the objection to observe that almost without exception the fears are held by those who do not believe in decentralization as a policy of administration.

Decentralization frankly seeks to promote diversity; centralization requires uniformity and standardization.

It follows quite simply that if your idea of "co-ordination" is *national uniformity* in *administration*, regionalism *will* create insuperable problems of "co-ordination." If you cannot conceive of a well-governed country that in every region is not standardized, identical, and uniform, then you do not want decentralization, and of course you would be opposed to regional authorities. If, on the other hand, diversity under broad national policies rather than uniformity in administration, adaptation to regional differences, and discretion and flexibility through the broad reaches of this greatly varied country are what appeal to you as sound, humane, and desirable, then the problems of co-ordination that cause the centralizers such concern become relatively simple and manageable.

It is difficult to exaggerate the lengths to which some men with administrative responsibility feel it is necessary to go in order to secure what they call co-ordination. This extends to matters of managerial detail. What such men would mean by the "co-ordination" of methods of federal land-buying—I use this only by way of a wholly hypothetical illustration—would be to erase differences as to the methods that might exist between federal land buyers dealing with small upland farms in east Tennessee and those applied in the flat sectionalized reaches of northern Indiana. To them a regulation respecting personnel management is not a good regulation if it does not apply uniformly throughout this whole country.

Now if your mind operates that way you would be opposed to regionalism. For only a centralized government can pour the country into such a single mold. If differences in how a public program is administered in the Tennessee Valley and in the Arkansas Valley, in Illinois and in New Mexico, disturb you, if those differences appear to be a "conflict," then you are right in assuming that regional decentralization will promote conflict.

This is not to say that under regionalism there will not be conflicts between regions. The major ones of these conflicts must be decided by Congress, as they have been since the very establishment of our central government. Other major conflicts involving the Executive Department would have to be decided by the President, as they always have been under centralized government administration.

So long as we harbor the administrative obsession that uniformity in administration is essential, the amount of co-ordination of this kind with which Congress and the President must deal and must continue to deal will be very great. Nor will regionalism eliminate all or most of these conflicts. But I do venture the assertion that it will considerably lessen them. This is true because the best place to co-ordinate is *close to the point where the conflict arises,* and not in the top levels and central offices. Industrial managers know this and practice it daily. The same thing proves true in government.

And so, looking at the whole picture, it can be said with confidence that in the national interest the difficulties of co-ordination are certainly not increased, and I think upon consideration it will be seen that they are actually diminished, by regionalism. Let the reader reflect upon the way in which the TVA has brought into the task of resource development a great host of local communities and state agencies. The problems of co-ordinating these efforts have not proved to be insuperable because TVA is a decentralized federal agency operating in the Tennessee Valley region with power to make its decisions in the field. The serious conflicts in administration are the ones which, unresolved in the local communities, find their way into the remote and often unreal atmosphere where men are dealing in "jurisdiction" and, as I have said, are preoccupied with their own institutions.

Co-ordination between a regional agency and other federal regional agencies or centralized departments is not, of course, automatic. The TVA has, from the outset, developed a comprehensive scheme of active co-operation with every other federal agency, either in Washington or in field offices, that has a responsibility or a function which could be helpful in the building of this region. In an earlier chapter I have alluded to the extent to which the changes in this valley have been due to these other federal activities; I wish to repeat and emphasize that here. The TVA has entered into hundreds of contracts with more than a score of other federal departments and bureaus. These inter-federal agency contracts and the relations carried on under them have from time to time developed serious differences on matters of importance. The task of reaching agreement has not always been an easy one. Yet there has never been any difference that could not be worked out, usually between the staffs of the agencies. In ten years no conflict between the TVA and these many federal departments and bureaus has made necessary a single conference with the President. In fact, the TVA Board has on only one occasion found it necessary to confer with the President on Authority problems in the three and a half years since the fall of France and the ensuing conversion of TVA to war needs.

The subject of regionalism has the widest ramifications, since it touches fundamental issues; a complete discussion is beyond the scope of this book. But our experience indicates clearly that the asserted danger of conflicts and the difficulties of coordination arising from regional decentralization are exaggerated and largely unreal.

Chapter 16

MODERN TOOLS FOR A MODERN JOB

A NEW and modern task requires new and modern tools; a spirit of enterprise and a creative modern outlook are quite as necessary in devising the mechanics of getting things done as in establishing policies and goals. What the TVA set out to do was such a new and modern task. For such an undertaking Congress and the President invented an entirely new kind of government implement: the regional development corporation.

This corporate public agency, the Tennessee Valley Authority, was thus set up to be as different in its organization and the way it was to do its work as the scope and the nature of the task it was directed to do was different from previous American efforts in resource development. It is not, however, the fact that the TVA was cast in the mold of a corporation that is distinctive. The corporate device for public undertakings was, of course, neither new nor unique.

The TVA is a significant departure as an instrument of twentieth-century democracy in this: that, in creating the TVA, Congress adopted and carefully wrote into law the basic principles and practices of modern management. A federal agency with the broadest of responsibilities was given a full set of the tools that American business has found essential to good management.

There have been few pieces of legislation in which so much consideration has been given, through long Congressional committee hearings and debates on the floor, to principles of management and the kind of organization needed to carry out a new national policy. This in itself is an event of importance, rare in American government annals, and one that made easier our task of translating the law into results.

In even the most carefully considered legislation, where the policy issues may be extensively debated, the method proposed for accomplishing the policies is seldom given attention. Frequently the administrative provisions of a proposed law, which may make effective or doom to failure the policies so hotly contested, are prepared by some drafting clerk, who simply copies the language of some earlier law or bill that seems to him to present a rough analogy. Or quite as frequently the method of administration finds its way into the bill not to promote the purposes of the proposed legislation, not because it is custom-built to promote the specific objectives of the bill, but upon the urging of some existing government agency eager to expand the field of its jurisdiction or to protect "vested" bureau rights.

The stupefying complexity of government procedure, the overcentralization and the multiplicity of "clearances" and approvals required before anything can be done, have bred intolerable delays, jurisdictional rows, and the practice of "passing the buck." These can be traced in considerable part to inattention to these potential evils when the devil's brew is being cooked, in the course of the legislative process. This failure to recognize the importance of principles of modern management in public affairs may bring upon us the gravest consequences in the immediate future.

For a host of new difficulties face us, as soon as the war is over, and indeed even before hostilities actually cease: the disposition of many billions of dollars' worth of the most modern industrial plants owned by the government; establishment of the mechanics of trade with other countries, the economic instruments of maintaining peaceful relations in the world; intensive resource development within our country—the list will be a long and varied one. The problems will not be traditional but as new and modern as the hydro-electric works, the huge cargo planes, and the electronic devices that will revolutionize the setting in which the world will function. It is all too likely, unless past lassitude and unawareness can be changed, that the *implements* to make effective the policies determined upon for these modern issues will be traditional, hidebound, creaky.

The TVA, then, affords a demonstration of a truth that needs full understanding in these days when vague abstractions fill the post-war planning atmosphere: that the *method* of getting a job done is of the greatest consequence, and not to be ignored or passed over casually. Further, the choice of method will determine whether resource development and industrialization, public or private, will be dictatorial—for the benefit of some especially privileged "elite," economic or political—or will be democratic—with the people actively participating and deriving the benefits.

A task cannot be done democratically if the method chosen for doing it is bureaucratic. And by this I mean performed exclusively by members of a bureau, governmental or private, whereby things are done "to" people, not with them. An undertaking cannot nourish a democratic spirit in men if, by law or custom, it must be carried out in a bureaucratic way.

The choice of tools is vital. The choice may be such that makes it impossible to decentralize and bring the experts and responsible administrators close to the people, where they must share the people's problems. The method chosen may thwart any hope of achieving unity in the development of resources because the agency of development is not permitted to adopt management practices that will effect that unity. Method is not a dull matter of "administration"; it is as inseparable from purpose and ends as our flesh is from our blood.

The reasons why the laws creating bureaus, commissions, and departments have, by almost invariable custom, failed to follow modern principles of management are not too difficult to understand. The policies of lawmaking in the immediate past have been largely regulatory and negative: "This shall *not* be done." The atmosphere of the legislature has therefore been heavy with this regulatory spirit, expressed in carefully limited responsibility, lack of trust, and forever setting one man to watch and checkmate another.

The tradition and climate of the skill of management, however, are remote from all such negation. Management is affirmative and initiatory: "This *is* to be done." It is in the process of defining, with skill and sense, what is to be done, and with it the *fixing of responsibility* for results, with wide freedom for judgment in the managers as to how it may best be done, that you have the essence of the best modern management.

In TVA's charter Congress stated clearly what was to be done in the Tennessee Valley: idle resources were to be set to work—rivers, land, minerals, forests. The job to be done was defined, clearly, simply, and yet in broad, inclusive terms. Navigation: a 9-foot minimum channel, from Knoxville to the Ohio. Flood control on the Tennessee and lower Mississippi. Power: the maximum consistent with other uses of the river's water. Agricultural and industrial development, operation of the Muscle Shoals plant, research, and so on. Congress told TVA's administrators what was expected of us, and by what measure we would be judged and held accountable.

Not only *what* was to be done but the fundamental policies we were to follow were likewise set out. Thus, as to the disposition of electricity, Congress did not attempt to handle the business detail of fixing the particular rates to be charged, but directed the policy TVA should observe in fixing those rates. We were not instructed by law as to where dams should be built, nor was their daily operation prescribed. We were told, however, that certain broad policies should govern in their construction and operation; e.g., they must be multiple in purpose, and flood control and navigation should have priority over power production if there were conflict. TVA's detailed financial records were not prescribed, but policies of financing and cost keeping were defined. Who was to be employed and how selected were not written into our charter, but employment, it was stipulated, must be solely upon merit and without political considerations. A policy of democratic methods in administration was encouraged, by repeated authorization in the law for co-operation with existing state and local agencies, with farmers and farm groups, with public and non-profit organizations. But the precise manner in which these and other policies should be carried out was not fixed.

Such is the method of good business management. Most agencies of government, however, new as well as old, have not been thus dealt with by Congress. Although no private board of directors would determine details of management—how much, for example, could be expended on such an item as travel cost—that is just the practice generally followed in the annual appropriations for federal establishments. The exact dollar amount, which may not be exceeded, for thousands of detailed managerial items of cost is fixed by law. Operating the details of a huge enterprise in this way is, of course, not in line with modern business management. This practice, in the case of an enterprise such as the TVA, would distort and magnify out of all proportion these separate elements of the task represented by the fixed items of appropriation. The administrator who should be concentrating upon the best way to obtain the over-all result is, by reason of particularized statutory limitations and managerial directions, necessarily distracted and preoccupied with items of detail rather than with the results of the whole undertaking. The unifying and generalizing function of management—its vital role—is deadened by the pressures and confusions of clinical details that have thus been given the dignity of legal mandate.

Such detailed direction has not been the Congressional practice followed in respect to the TVA, except in one instance in 1942, when the maximum expenditure for travel was fixed by law, against TVA's recommendation. This departure from modern management principles, offered in all sincerity as an economy measure, actually resulted in higher costs and waste; any good manager will see why this was inevitable. Less than a year later Congress reconsidered and itself rescinded its action; steps were authorized to correct the error and these were made retroactive. It became apparent to the legislators that in the TVA the cost of keeping personnel in the field (in traditional government terminology called "travel cost") is but one item of many that go into the cost of building a dam or transmission line, or operating a chemical plant.

The job having been defined and the broad policies laid down, Congress in the TVA Act did what is new in our history: it fixed upon one agency the responsibility for results in resource development in a region. What seems the plainest sense to a manager, i.e., fixing responsibility in one place for an entire undertaking of many parts, all interrelated and interwoven— land, water, minerals, forests—was virtually a revolution in government administration.

In the development of the river, not flood control alone, or navigation or power, but all the water's uses, together, were to be the responsibility of one public agency. Not water resources in one compartment of government, dealt with separately from soil or forests, nor farming separately from industry, nor industry separate from transport and electricity. The TVA's responsibilities for results were to be measured by the concept of the unity of resources. TVA's corporate charter makes this plain not only by the specific directions given but also by the indication of a broad purpose expressed in such statutory language as the following: "To aid further the proper use, conservation and development of the natural resources of the Tennessee River drainage basin . . ."; "the economic and social well-being of the people living in said river basin"; "physical, economic and social development of said areas"; "provide for the agricultural and industrial development of said Valley," and the like.

The best antidote for buck-passing and alibis for failure to get results is the fixing of responsibility. Regrettably, this well-established principle appears to be still a novelty in many areas of public administration. It was by thus fixing responsibility that Congress cut off any excuse by which TVA might escape accountability. If the building of the dams created a public health hazard from malaria, say, it was no excuse for TVA to reply that public health was the responsibility of some other agency. If in the use of the river to produce power, floods were not adequately controlled, there was no alibi available that flood control was someone else's responsibility. If power costs were too high to permit liquidation of the investment, there was no escaping accountability because someone else built the dams inefficiently. Similarly with the everyday matters of management—the selection of personnel, for example.

The Board of TVA and not the Civil Service Commission, by a specific provision of the Authority's charter, was made responsible for the employment, promotion, and discharge of all its personnel, from general manager to messenger boy. We were to establish what the law called a "merit" system, and we did; but if the men selected were incompetent or insensitive to the people's problems, or if it took a month to employ a stenographer or lineman when it needed to be done in a day, we could not try to pass the blame to the Civil Service Commission's rules, nor could our supervisors escape their accountability to the TVA Board in that way. The notion that the TVA Board was to be entrusted, for example, with the building of the Kentucky Dam, costing $110,000,000, but not with employing the men who were to design and build it seems fantastic. And yet so rarely does our government follow the ordinary practices of fixing responsibility that, as of the time I write, TVA is the *only* permanent federal agency that remains solely responsible for the selection and promotion of its personnel.

Senator Lister Hill, who in 1933 as a Representative was one of the conference managers for the original bill, said in a recent communication to the Senate Judiciary Committee that it was

the intent of the whole [TVA] statute—to create an agency which would be free of some of the Government red tape about which we complain, which would have authority commensurate with its responsibilities. We made certain that it could not "pass the buck" to another bureau or department in the event of failure, and that it would not be required to waste time and energy in jurisdictional disputes. It was intended that the Board alone be held responsible for the effective administration of the policies laid down by Congress.

Congress was consistent in extending this managerial principle of fixed and undivided responsibility to include the everyday operations of the undertaking. Land buying for TVA reservoirs (including examination of titles and condemnation where necessary), for example, is not separated from the rest of the task and put in other hands, which is the general federal practice. If the land is not acquired rapidly enough to meet the construction schedules of the dam builders, or if the land owners are not fairly, speedily, or courteously dealt with, the TVA Board cannot blame any other agency of government. And so with the purchase of machinery, supplies, etc., and the settlement of damage or contract claims against TVA. Such managerial functions in most government undertakings are detached from those who are in charge of individual tasks—buildings, plants, dams, etc.—and centralized in several separate and independent agencies which do not have responsibility for the *total* result. To business managers accustomed to quite different methods, this splitting up of a single task is a source of constant frustration in their dealing with the government.

Following the principles of sound management, Congress, despite persistent proposals to the contrary by antagonists of the Authority, has declined to relieve TVA of responsibility for the legality and appropriateness of its expenditures, and this position meets with the approval of the incumbent Comptroller General of the United States, who audits the TVA's accounts on behalf of Congress. Thus TVA is given managerial discretion but is held strictly accountable not only for what it does but for *how well* it does it.

Such fixing of responsibility increases initiative and gives an opportunity for enterprise and experiment. The field of co-operative labor relations is one example. Every modern management knows that achieving good results in a difficult undertaking depends largely upon a working relation with employees that establishes confidence and fosters enthusiasm and zest for the task. A strike or any interruption of work on TVA's power system or upon a dam under construction would be a catastrophe for which TVA administrators would be held solely responsible. The development of productive labor relations, therefore, became one of our major concerns at the very outset.

Active labor-management co-operation between organized workers and the TVA, now widely known and generally approved, could never have come about if Congress had provided for any division of responsibility for personnel management as between TVA's management and some other agency. Fixing of responsibility has thereby furthered "administrative democracy," in those vital relations between TVA management and employees. It should be obvious that, unless *within TVA* democratic methods are followed (not only as between labor and management but within TVA's management itself), it is impossible to expect that TVA can further strengthen the democratic spirit in the life of the valley.

Congress refused to divide responsibility in the TVA undertaking because it may have seen that such a course has in the past inevitably produced a senseless uniformity, and its offspring, rigidity and sterility. For, when functions are thus severed from the main body of responsibility that nourishes them and gives them life and reality, any agency thus exercising disembodied authority must attempt to write "regulations" detailed enough to prevent mistakes and abuses of discretion. And, since such rules are commonly prescribed on a nation-wide basis to secure the fancied benefits of standardization, the lowest common denominator of conduct inevitably governs. The rituals of regulations, jurisdictional disputes, and the glorification of red tape thrive in such an atmosphere of divided responsibility.

I am not implying, of course, that there is anything peculiar about American public service. In Great Britain in the adminis-

tration of government functions the British Civil Service, sometimes described as the best in the world, has shown the same
tendencies, where management principles have not been applied.
An observer makes this comment on conventional governmental
methods in Britain, indicating how universal are these matters:

The civil service tradition [in Great Britain] implies a rigid hier-
archical organization of authority. . . . The possibility of Parlia-
mentary interpellation upon any detail of administration crystallises
rigidity and overcentralization; an ex-Postmaster-General declares
that as a result of this direct legislative control, "the minutiae of
administration come right up to the highest officials, diverting their
minds from broad matters of policy." However well suited to routine
administration, the complete security of tenure characterising the
civil service, with a tendency to promotion by seniority rather than
merit, probably fails to offer an adequate spur to expression or orig-
inality, a first necessity in broadcasting, or to the salesmanship
needed to create demand for a service.*

A distinguished Manchester businessman with extensive experience in public affairs, Sir Ernest Simon, on a visit to the TVA
in 1943, commented upon the spirit of initiative in the TVA staff.
He has since summarized his firsthand observations in this valley
in a printed statement which reads in part:

The [TVA] Directors . . . have done all they can to delegate responsibility right down through the staff . . . [and] to cut out Civil
Service red tape and the spirit of bureaucracy. The whole staff is
encouraged to take responsibility, and not to worry if they make mistakes. The Directors have managed, I think, to get a spirit of construc-
tive initiative throughout the staff as good as anything in the best
private businesses.

Whatever the shortcomings in TVA's management, whatever
delays, waste, and operating inefficiency there have been, is the
direct responsibility of the Board of TVA itself. For Congress
provided the conditions for us that make competent management possible. The attitude of Congress and the President toward

* Gordon, *The Public Corporation in Great Britain* (London: Oxford
University Press, 1938), p. 321.

us has been substantially that of a good business corporation toward its management. "Here's your job. Here is the broad method we expect you to follow. On managerial detail it is up to you to pick the best way, within the framework of the policies of your charter. You are the manager. Get the job done. If you cannot and do not, you and you alone will be held responsible."

The corporation is a vehicle well adapted to such fixing of responsibility. The fact that TVA was set up as a corporation, however, is not alone any guarantee that it would not be subjected to the same rituals of divided responsibility, clearances, and detailed management by Congress as any bureau; in fact, some of our public corporations are thus encumbered. But, while no guarantee, there was a psychological advantage in using the corporate device, since by established practice and custom the corporation has come to embody in people's minds this idea of managerial responsibility.

Congress in 1933 took advantage of the opportunity that its selection of the independent corporate device created, and freed the TVA of the conventional procedures of government agencies and bureaus. The TVA continues in this autonomous status; it is not part of any of the existing bureaus and departments, and the head of the TVA reports directly to the President and to Congress.

Suppose these principles of management and decentralization, which Congress made it possible for TVA to put into effect in this valley, should be extended throughout the government. Would it mean the virtual abolition of the historic departments in Washington? How would it affect existing bureaus? Discussion of these and similar questions is beyond the scope of this book. But it should be evident that, even if these principles were extended to every federal activity to which they could appropriately be applied, many central departmental and bureau functions would be entirely unaffected. It is also evident that the size of some of the Washington departments would be reduced, and the nature and character of the work they perform would change.

I hope these questions concerning management in government will be the subject of study and objective discussion. For the questions are going to be asked. Our federal government will be increasingly the subject of critical study by Congress and the people; experimentation and change (some of it drastic) are inevitable.

The people's everyday life has now become too intimately related to the way the government functions for the subject to be longer regarded as the exclusive field of professionals. Standpatters within government can sometimes manage to make official life uncomfortable and abbreviated for the many administrators and managers who insist that there can be no such thing as a personal or political vested right in established government practice, however venerable; but this will not stem the tide of the public's demand that their government adopt the essentials of modern management.

Chapter 17

WHAT ABOUT "POLITICS"?

CAN politics be kept out of TVA?
This is a question that is often asked and has been extensively debated. By "politics" people mean nothing vague nor abstract. They mean such things as these: the appointment of engineers, land buyers, and workmen because they (or their friends or relatives) have helped to elect certain men to office; the preparation of specifications in a way that will favor the bid of some manufacturer who is politically "right"; the location of dams where they will win the most votes; in short, the use of TVA for partisan political purposes.

Opponents of the TVA during the long years of debate insisted that it was inevitable that partisan politics would infect TVA, and indeed any government undertaking of this character. This was in fact one of the chief arguments leveled against the proposals for a publicly owned enterprise as urged by Senator Norris. To prevent these forebodings from becoming a reality has been an important preoccupation of the administrators of the project. That we have been thus far successful is due largely to the decision of Congress itself that politics must be kept out, a decision written into the explicit language of the law.

A river has no politics. Whether an engineer is a Democrat or a Republican, a conservative or a liberal, or indeed whether he has any interest in or knowledge of political matters at all, is entirely unrelated to his ability to design a dam. In this sense, experts as well as rivers have no politics. But the question of whether a river should be developed *is* a political question, and

179

hence a proper subject of "politics." Whether a series of dams should provide only navigation, or instead should serve all the unified purposes to which the river can be put—this *is* a political question, and should be decided by Congress. The TVA Act is filled with such broad political decisions, made, as they should and must be made, by the elected representatives of the whole people. The decision to develop resources as a unified whole was a political one; the opportunity afforded for regional decentralization, the fixing of responsibility on a single agency in a region, even the decision that TVA must keep politics out of the selection of personnel—all these were political decisions.

Facts and experienced judgment, not political views, are the foundation of dependable technical decisions and action. Whether the rock at a particular site is a safe dam foundation or whether a certain kind of truck or transmission tower is best fitted for a job—these are not political questions and should not be decided politically or by political bodies. And, conversely, experts and administrators should not directly or by indirection decide political issues; moreover it is vital that they be held strictly answerable for their performance to prevailing public opinion, as expressed from time to time through democratic political methods.

Are these compatible principles? *Can science and politics live together* without one dominating the other? Can experts and managers be kept accountable to the public despite the great power over the lives of all of us that technical knowledge puts in their hands?

The TVA has, of course, inevitably faced these fundamental questions many times in the past ten years. The answers thus far have been in the affirmative. It is quite generally conceded that a high standard of technical and managerial competence has been maintained, and that the TVA has been guided by public policies laid down by Congress. It has remained responsive to the wishes of the people it serves, who warmly support TVA's resistance to political interference. The words used by

Senator Bankhead of Alabama in a recent Senate debate fairly summarize the situation:

> The TVA has no political activities; it has no policy-making programs except to carry out those declared in the Act, and they have been carried out to the very general satisfaction, as we have heard from all sides . . .
>
> In the Tennessee Valley, regardless of politics, the program has the approval of the people, and the effort to bring under the confirmation power of the Senate [embodied in a bill to which the Senator was addressing himself] the engineers and architects and accountants and others connected with TVA is bitterly resisted by the people . . .
>
> I have not heard a word from any citizen in the whole Tennessee Valley in favor of the proposed program [respecting Senate confirmation], but, on the contrary, countless letters, by the hundreds, possibly by the thousands, have come to me in opposition to any such program as that proposed, which would have a tendency to indicate that the TVA is to be made a political organization.

No broad conclusions about politics in its relation to technology, however, should be drawn from TVA's successful course in this respect in its first ten years. It is always within the power of Congress to change the policy of keeping politics out of TVA. As a matter of fact the bill condemned by Senator Bankhead did pass the Senate in June, 1943, and as I write is still pending before a Committee of the House of Representatives. The issue, even as to TVA, may never be safely deemed as "settled."

Public understanding is the only possible safeguard against the mixing of politics and technology, and against the parallel evil of lack of accountability of administrators to the people. Considerations of theory will hardly determine whether the policy thus far successful in the TVA will be applied and followed in other comparable fields of public technical and managerial activities. Such public understanding must be constantly refreshed by concrete instances of the wisdom of the right course and the high cost of the wrong one.

This is no abstract question of "political science." In the immediate future America will be faced with major decisions that involve this very issue—questions, for example, concerning the disposition of government-owned plane factories, aluminum, rubber, chemical and steel works, shipyards, and the like—investments running into many billions of dollars. Will the many technical questions be decided by political methods? On the other hand, will experts and industrial managers seek to disguise underlying policy questions by calling them "technical" or "economic," and thereby themselves decide political issues? Will these problems be dealt with in a kind of free-for-all fight between politics and managerial and technical judgment? The light of TVA's analogous experience is here of not a little practical importance.

As I have previously indicated, the appointment of all TVA officers and employees was vested exclusively in the hands of the Board of Directors. By an unusual provision Congress expressly excluded political considerations in all such appointments. The language was forthright: "No political test or qualification shall be permitted or given consideration, but all such appointments and promotions shall be given and made on the basis of merit and efficiency." Violation of this provision subjects a member of the Board of Directors to removal from office by the President and any employee to removal by the TVA Board. Under this authorization a complete system of personnel selection was set up, based upon methods that have been generously commended in managerial circles in both public and private business. Because custom-built for the special needs and circumstances under which TVA operates, this personnel system was able to meet the strain of a sudden and huge expansion due to war needs. Thus TVA's total force increased, owing to the emergency need for power and munitions, from approximately 14,000 in 1940 to 40,000 in 1942; four days after one emergency dam was authorized by Congress on January 30, 1942, the Personnel Department had some 1,800 men and women on the job. All this work of personnel selection has been carried on outside both the patronage system and the Civil Service.

At the outset there was a disposition on the part of some Members of Congress to ask us to disregard or evade this explicit provision against political appointments. When it became evident, however, that we intended to hew consistently to the line, and that there would be no exceptions, the initial impatience diminished. After a trying year or two the policy came to be well recognized and generally accepted. Many Members of Congress have expressed approval of the policy.

What Senator Barkley of Kentucky (the majority leader) said on the floor of the Senate recently is representative of the experience and the position of many legislators:

Mr. President, I have had my moments of disagreement and impatience growing out of perfectly natural and human reactions on account of the Tennessee Valley Authority. When the Gilbertsville Dam [now known as the Kentucky Dam] was authorized and construction of it was begun, unemployment was rife and widespread in the Tennessee Valley region and in my State. I live within 23 miles of the Gilbertsville Dam. Thousands of persons came to me thinking that I could obtain employment for them in the Tennessee Valley Authority. To all of them I pointed out the fact that when we enacted the law in the beginning we were so anxious to keep the TVA out of politics that we put in the law a provision that no political consideration should be given by the Tennessee Valley Authority to the employment of any person who might apply for employment under it.

The TVA has been so anxious to obey that injunction of the Congress and to be meticulous in the observance of that law that a recommendation by a Member of the Senate or the House was a disadvantage rather than an advantage to those who sought employment. The Tennessee Valley Authority did not want the people to get the idea that anybody could come there and obtain a job because he had a letter from a Senator or Representative. . . . I mention that because the TVA has been kept absolutely out of politics. It has given no consideration to politics in employing anybody, whether he was a Democrat, Republican, or otherwise.

The Senator then proceeded to express his strong opposition to legislation that he believed would inject politics into TVA. To retain technicians and managers of high caliber would have been impossible if it had not been for this policy. But far more is at stake than the appointment and promotion of employees on their merits. An employee who owes his appointment to his political standing is a man whose allegiance is not solely to the merits and the public purposes of the undertaking. The whole enterprise would be infected by half-technical, half-political judgments. There would be no foundation upon which TVA could stand. Public confidence in its integrity would soon fade. Once politics enters, the entire edifice of an enterprise built upon expert skills becomes unsafe.

Now there are of course all kinds of "politics." Administrators and technicians, however high-minded their purposes may seem to them, cannot piously abjure party politics, and then indulge in their own variety. "Taking care of the boys" is an evil in any guise, whether it is on the basis of personal friendship, business or social ties, or some amateur political notion about an "elite of brains" (self-selected), a kind of Phi Beta Kappa version of Tammany Hall.

The usual forthrightness of Congressmen is wholesome compared with the "holier-than-thou" attitude toward politicians of those who occasionally practice their own personal brand of politics. I was reminded of this hypocrisy a few years ago, when I read a signed magazine editorial which denounced the political patronage system, in the most righteous terms. The writer of this piece is a man who in 1933 had been a powerful figure in the government. When TVA was first created this Galahad sent word to our Board that we must put one of his relatives on our pay roll. A jaunty young satellite brought us the message. We made the same reply that we had been giving to similar requests from Members of Congress: Let the relative file his application and be judged along with other applicants. The messenger tried to wave all this aside. He had been told (he said) to let us know that such rules about examinations were not intended to apply to men of such high social purposes! Both of these men have long since discredited themselves and are out of public service, but before this happened they had done not a little damage to the reputation for disinterestedness of all public administrators.

The employment of relatives is a form of personal politics; one of TVA's first actions was to establish a strong policy against the practice of nepotism. And then there are those businessmen who come into the government to perform a technical job of war production who find nothing incongruous in injecting into a conference a partisan attack on the President or Members of Congress, or who even use a government post to further a particular political candidacy—these too are men who surely fail to comprehend the harm they are doing to public confidence in technicians in public affairs. There are all kinds of politics; administrators and experts must see to it that they keep out of all varieties.

Congress itself determined to keep its kind of politics out of TVA's technical administration. It was, in turn, our responsibility as administrators to keep TVA out of political matters. Accordingly TVA in 1936 adopted a policy forbidding political activity by anyone connected with the TVA, even in municipal affairs. No TVA employee could be a candidate for any office, or be active in elections of any kind, except of course, to vote. This was a number of years before the Hatch Act placed similar but less extensive limits upon political activity of all federal employees. It is arguable that the TVA's policy is too extreme in that it forbids thousands of citizens living in the Tennessee Valley from useful participation in strictly community governmental affairs, but on balance we feel this restriction is justified by the dangers it averts.

TVA, if it were politically managed, could become a curse to this valley. Just what would it mean if politics had been injected into TVA's selection of personnel, or into detailed administration of funds by which the job is carried out? It would mean that the thousands of miles of transmission lines built by TVA's forces might have been located not for economic and engineering reasons, but upon a political basis. A city that votes "right," a county that delivers the "right" number of votes for a particular organization or candidate, an industry that "comes through," could be rewarded by advantages in the location of transmission lines, though such a location was not justified by the business facts. A city and its industries that do not vote "right" might find that its electric substations were not adequately maintained, that service was poor, that its industrial growth had stopped. Even if these things never actually happened, the disintegrating suspicion that politics was under the surface would always be there.

If the TVA were under political management its transactions for purchase of materials and equipment—tens of thousands of contracts totaling hundreds of millions of dollars, every one awarded on business principles of cost and relative quality of products—would have been potential political rewards. Even the location of dams might be the subject of political decisions rather than based on streamflow, character of the foundation, cost compared with other sites, and similar factual engineering considerations. Indeed in one recent instance TVA earned very costly political opposition because it persisted in recommending the location of a dam solely upon such facts.

In the spring of 1942 a bill was introduced into Congress to change TVA's method of financing in such a way as to inject political considerations into the technical and business operations of TVA. Public understanding of this issue of politics in TVA took on unprecedented forms. Full-page advertisements protesting against the measure appeared in the daily papers, sponsored by and paid for by the valley's Chambers of Commerce and local service clubs. The valley press almost unanimously expressed strong opposition in repeated editorials. The bill was even opposed by a national magazine which speaks for the private electric industry and opposed the creation of TVA: "TVA has a trained personnel and a competent engineering staff operating under a capable management . . . TVA should be free from political control."[1] The theme of the newspaper advertising, the letters, the editorials, the resolutions of Sunday-

[1] *Electrical World*, May 16, 1943, pp. 56-7.

school classes and women's clubs was: "Keep politics out of TVA." The proposal, like earlier ones to similar effect, was not enacted.

It is accurate to say that TVA has demonstrated to the satisfaction of those most directly affected that the task of getting resources developed should be kept non-political. It is now "good politics" for political leaders themselves, in the Tennessee Valley, to urge that politics be kept out of TVA. Probably the most thoughtful and informed leadership on the basic issues of the valley's development is coming from a group of its younger political leaders and elected officials. They know that their support of TVA will not be rewarded by jobs or favors, and have long since ceased to think in those terms. If TVA does a good job, one that the valley and the country judges to be competent, that constitutes their political reward. And to the surprise of many "realistic" people, it turns out that helping to keep politics out of TVA is a political asset to candidates for public office in the valley. It is another case where "no politics is good politics." As long as the people these elected officials represent have confidence in the TVA idea and the technical and managerial craftsmanship behind it, the danger of politics in administration is not great; whenever that is lost, the injection of political decisions and methods is not far off.

But it would not be safe or wise to give to the administrators of the TVA such broad independence of action in carrying out political decisions made by Congress unless they were held strictly accountable for results. (And what is true of TVA seems to me applicable to managers and experts generally.) Moreover, TVA's freedom from interference in carrying out policies determined by Congress makes it imperative that the policies themselves be under constant control and review by Congress as the instrument of politics. When managers and technicians, in business or in government, are permitted to use the leverage of their authority and expert knowledge to lodge irresponsible power in themselves, the foundation of democracy is threatened at once.

Accountability begins with a full report of results. The TVA each year makes several such reports, public documents with a wide circulation. The Authority's regular report of its activities, made annually to Congress, is in great detail. Reports on special subjects are made from time to time. Financial reporting is comprehensive; it embodies the most progressive business methods: detailed unit cost accounting; a monthly and annual financial statement, including balance sheet and income account; an audit not only by the Comptroller General of the United States, but in addition by a leading firm of commercial accountants, whose report attached to TVA's annual financial reports is in much the same language as the certification the same firm appends to the financial statements of some of America's largest private concerns. An elaborate accounting of results is also made each year before the Appropriations Committees of both Houses of Congress, as well as to the President through the Bureau of the Budget. Such reports as these have been the occasion of extensive debate over TVA in Congress, in the press, and in other public forums.

There are few enterprises, public or private, which have been subjected to more vigorous and persistent public review or about which more detailed reports have been made. Thus in 1938 a Joint Congressional Committee to investigate the TVA, equipped with a considerable technical staff, spent a year investigating the TVA. Its report, proceedings, and engineering analysis totaled 7,500 printed pages.

From time to time the entire TVA program has been reviewed in Congress in the course of consideration of statutory amendments or appropriations. In the ensuing hearings and debate the effectiveness of its management has been inquired into, new public policies have been written into TVA's basic charter, existing ones confirmed. In 1938, for example, a contract entered into by the TVA to purchase properties of the Tennessee Electric Power Company was reviewed by Congress. Every question in a lengthy contract, on which Mr. Wendell Willkie (on behalf of the company) and I had spent years of negotiation, was thus publicly examined, debated, and confirmed. Another instance of Congressional review of policy occurred in 1940 when the law respecting tax payments by TVA was changed. The committee hearings in Congress and the debates constituted a reappraisal of fundamental policy and an accounting of stewardship by TVA's managers covering virtually every phase of the enterprise.

It has been demonstrated by these and other instances that it is entirely feasible to hold this public enterprise to strict accountability and responsibility without resort to political controls of the details of operation from the floor of Congress. But it is in far less formal ways that the most effective responsibility to the people is established. *Working at the grass roots is the surest guarantee of that day-to-day adjustment to the needs and aspirations of the people which is the liveliest form of public accountability.* When the managers and the experts are close to the people and their problems, it does not ordinarily take the formality of a Congressional hearing to determine whether the program undertaken is succeeding or needs adjustment, whether staff members are alive to their opportunities or are arrogant and self-seeking.

Decentralization is a kind of mirror in which one can see, each day and each hour, how well or how badly the work responds to its broad purpose. Because it is a regional agency, doing its work and making its decisions in the valley, TVA cannot escape the sight of its mistakes or irresponsibly turn its back upon the stream of daily life. Success can come only through a technical leadership in which the people, not in the mysterious aura of distance but under the revealing and commonplace light of proximity and familiarity, have confidence. At the grass roots a new kind of accountability is born, more significant than reports, reviews, criticism by Congress. It is the day-to-day accountability of working partner to working partner.

Will the managers and experts of business and government enterprises, whose skills give them such great power, become a new ruling class, exploiting the rest of society for their own benefit? In a widely discussed book, *The Managerial Revolution,* Professor James Burnham asserts that such a "drive for social dominance, for power and privilege, for the position of ruling class by the social group or class of managers"[2] has already taken place in Germany and Russia, and, so Professor Burnham states, is far along on its inevitable way in the United States. The functions of our "new masters," Burnham says, are now being performed in the earlier stages of this "managerial revolution" by the executives of enterprises of which he singles out General Motors and the Tennessee Valley Authority as examples.

In the past, similar predictions have been made, predictions likewise adorned with analogies drawn from nations that are without the experience or talent for democracy that exists in this country. But what gives Burnham's restatement of this thesis its present importance is that it has been taken in dead seriousness by many men in managerial and technical posts. The idea of managerial domination cannot be lightly written off. The amount of influence which so cynical a thesis can have upon the vain, the naïve, and the impatient is not to be discounted. I trust it is clear that the methods of TVA are calculated to promote that accountability of the manager and that diffusion of power which are the precise opposite and may well be an effective antidote to the "managerial revolution."

More hazardous to democracy than such a dream of a ruling elite of managers and technicians, but not unrelated to it, is a growing contempt of "politics" and of Congress. This is nothing new or surprising from defeatists about democracy, and from reactionary forces generally. But to find this deprecation of politics spreading among progressives and especially among those who are administrators and technicians is a sign of great danger. The strongest expressions of disgust and impatience with politics and with Congress I have ever heard have come recently from men of great executive or technical ability in government service and in business who tried to get an urgent war job done

[2] (New York: John Day Co., 1941)

quickly, only to be delayed and even frustrated by what they describe as "political pressure," by exhausting Congressional committee hearings, and endless conferences with legislators. To overworked and conscientious men this is trying, of course. And it is true that when the line I have tried to draw in this chapter is crossed—the line between political policy-making and administrative execution of that policy—there is ample cause for this discouragement. But progressives, and especially those in administrative or technical posts, are under a peculiarly heavy responsibility to recognize, with scrupulous care, the role of politics in the fixing of basic policies. We must be the first to see that, if the institution of politics becomes discredited, the enemies of democracy have won an important victory.

Chapter 18

PLANNING AND PLANNERS

TVA is supposed to be a planning agency for this region. Yet nowhere on your organization chart do I find a Department of Social Planning; and when I ask for a copy of the TVA Plan no one can produce it: Some such comment has been made to us many times by friendly and earnest students of TVA.

The reason the TVA Plan is not available is that there is no such document. Nor is there one separate department set off by itself, where planners exercise their brains. To one who has read thus far in this account, it is evident this does not constitute our idea of planning.

The TVA *is* a planning agency, the first of its kind in the United States. The great change going on in this valley is an authentic example of modern democratic planning; this was the expressed intent of Congress, by whose authority we act. But through the years we have deliberately been sparing in the use of the terminology of "plans" and "planning" within TVA and outside, and those terms have hardly appeared thus far in this book. For the term "planning" has come to be used in so many different senses that the nomenclature has almost lost usefulness, has even come to be a source of some confusion.

It is necessary, however, to translate the ideas of this book into the terminology of planning and the language that planners employ. For planning ideas are widely discussed these days. To some the content of the word "planning" has been pared down until it means merely ordinary foresight, and thereby the term has lost any broad significance. Others have gone to the other extreme; they approve or violently condemn "planning" because to them it means a complete reconstitution of our social system, comprehensive state socialism, and the like. Some discerning and broad-gauge industrialists urge widespread "planning" for the post-war period; by this they mean a way of assuring the future of "free enterprise" or "democratic capitalism"—phrases that also have come by loose handling to be as foggy in their meaning as "planning" itself.

The term "planning," however, is here to stay; but, since it has apparently come to mean all things to all men, I have avoided using the term until I had set out specifically, as I have done in preceding chapters, just what I have in mind in using the word, and what planning means to us in this valley. "Unified development" as I have described the idea in action is, in substance, the valley's synonym for "planning."

We have always made plans in America. The question for us is not: Should we plan? but: *What kind of plans* should we make? What kind of planners? What method of "enforcement of plans"? On these matters what has transpired in the Tennessee Valley, as I have tried to describe it, casts the light of actual experience.

Economic and social planning in America is by no means new and strange, but is indeed as old as the Republic. Generally speaking, planning in this country in the past has been practiced by two great groups: first, by elected public officials, variously called "politicians" or "statesmen"; and, second, by businessmen, variously called "empire builders" or "exploiters of our resources."

Let us look for a moment at some of the instances of planning carried on by public men, selected to represent the economic interests and the social point of view of their constituents. Land planning, for example. By Royal Proclamation in 1763 the colonists were barred from free access to the western lands. Then, by the Ordinance of 1787, the politicians established a different conception of land planning: the opening of the western lands to settlers. The economic and social views of the people of that time called for land planning which would encourage and stimulate the settlement of the West.

Or take another illustration of public planning by elected officials, industrial planning. In the early days of American manufacturing, a plan was devised to stimulate industry. Certain of the public men of that day, like Hamilton and Webster and their sectional constituents, wanted a particular result: manufacturing in the Northeastern States. With the home market "protected," they planned an industrial future for the Northeast, and the method they used to effectuate the plan was the protective tariff.

The Homestead Act of 1862, the Income Tax Amendment, the Sherman Anti-Trust Act, the Granger Laws—one can recite instance after instance of public planning through our political institutions, through acts of Congress, acts of state legislatures, local ordinances.

One thing particularly characteristic of such planning by elected representatives is that they did not as a regular practice call into their councils the assistance of technically trained men —scientists, economists, engineers, administrators—to assist them in formulating these plans.

How well did these early planners do their job? Were the plans well conceived and in the public interest? This much is certain: their plans were not sterile, they were not merely reports and recommendations, written to be filed away and to gather dust. They were put into action, and out of that action in less than 150 years grew the greatest industrial and agricultural nation of all time.

Great as were some of the accomplishments of public planners in the past, we know that we suffer today from the consequences of some of those plans. The state of our natural resources has become a national emergency, grave and critical. Some of the public land policies embodied in such planning as the Homestead laws we now realize were short-sighted and costly. Such piecemeal planning for the immediate year-to-year

demands of particular groups of constituents we now know
was not wise planning. Catastrophic floods, denuded forests,
soil exhaustion—these are part of the price we are paying. For
a generation now a change in those plans has been urged. Overtones prophetic of President Roosevelt's message to Congress
concerning TVA were heard, faintly it is true, as early as 1909
when President Theodore Roosevelt's Conservation Commission made this recommendation:

Broad plans should be adopted providing for a system of waterway
improvement extending to all uses of the waters and benefits to be
derived from their control, including the clarification of the water and
abatement of floods for the benefit of navigation; the extension of
irrigation; the development and application of power; the prevention
of soil wash; the purification of streams for water supply; and the
drainage and utilization of the waters of swamp and overflow lands.

Discussion of industrial planning to enable America to grasp
the opportunities of the post-war period is now much in the
public prints, led by some of our ablest men of private business.
Here again, as in the case of planning by public men, we should
remember that when businessmen become planners they are not
venturing into new and strange fields. Long-range planning is
a familiar and established practice of progressive business. Perhaps the best-known example is that of the American Telephone
and Telegraph Company. This vast communication service has
expended large sums of money in continuous and intensive
study of the future, and on the basis of such study develops
plans five years, ten years, and even longer in advance—plans
for new construction, for the revision of its exchanges, for the
building of additional capacity. In other businesses there has
long been comparable economic planning with substantial
organizations devoted to the task. Surveys are made of the
market, financial trends, technological changes, all the complex
factors which will affect the future activities of a great business
enterprise.

Planning by businessmen, often under some other name, is

recognized as necessary to the conduct of private enterprise. It has the virtue of a single and direct objective, one that can be currently measured, that is, the making of a profit. A plan that is impressive in the form of a report but which does not work, as judged by the financial reports of the company, is an unsuccessful plan. It has been just as simple as that. The business planner has rarely felt it necessary to complicate his problem by trying to determine whether the making of profit under his plan benefits the whole of society, or injures it. And, as I have said, it is not often that a single business or even an entire industry is in a position to decide such a question.

This is admittedly a grave defect of planning by the businessman. For his legitimate object, namely a profitable business, is not necessarily consistent with the object of society, that is, a prosperous and happy people. The plans of the A. T. & T. and of the small manufacturer may both be quite effective within those enterprises. But factors affecting the plans of the A. T. & T. and the small manufacturer go far beyond their businesses. Over this multitude of external factors the businessman has no effective control. As this and a thousand valleys demonstrate so tragically, private planning, even when temporarily sound from the viewpoint of a particular enterprise, has often resulted in great injury to many other enterprises, and therefore to the public welfare.

The idea of unified resource development is based upon the premise that by democratic planning the individual's interest, the interest of private undertakings, can increasingly be made one with the interest of all of us, i.e., the community interest. By and large, things are working out that way in the Tennessee Valley. The income of the private business of farming has increased, largely as a result of a program of aiding the region's soil. Sales by private fertilizer companies have increased more rapidly than at any other time in their history as a result of TVA's production and the demonstration of new fertilizer products designed to further the over-all public interest in the land. Promotion of education in forest-fire protection and scientific cutting methods has furthered conservation and at the same time aided the private business of lumbering. Community planning has made towns more attractive and pleasant for everyone, and at the same time increased land values for individual owners. These results and many others I have described have been in the general public interest; all have furthered the interest of particular business enterprises.

Effective planners must understand and believe in people. The average man is constantly in the mind of the effective planning expert. Planners, whether they are technicians or administrators, must recognize that they are not dealing with philosophical abstractions, or mere statistics or engineering data or legal principles, and that planning is not an end in itself.

In the last analysis, in democratic planning it is human beings we are concerned with. Unless plans show an understanding and recognition of the aspirations of men and women, they will fail. Those who lack human understanding and cannot share the emotions of men can hardly forward the objectives of realistic planning. Thurman Arnold, in *The Symbols of Government,* has well described this type of earnest but unrealistic person:

They usually bungle their brief opportunities in power because they are too much in love with an ideal society to treat the one actually before them with skill and understanding. Their constant and futile cry is reiterated through the ages: "Let us educate the people so that they can understand and appreciate us."[1]

A great Plan, a moral and indeed a religious purpose, deep and fundamental, is democracy's answer both to our own home-grown would-be dictators and foreign anti-democracy alike. In the unified development of resources there is such a Great Plan: the Unity of Nature and Mankind. Under such a Plan in our valley we move forward. True, it is but a step at a time. But we assume responsibility not simply for the little advance we make each day, but for that vast and all-pervasive end and purpose of all our labors, the material well-being of all men

[1] (New Haven, Conn.: Yale University Press, 1935) pp. 21-2.

and the opportunity for them to build for themselves spiritual strength.

Here is the life principle of democratic planning— an awakening in the whole people of a sense of this common moral purpose. Not one goal, but a direction. Not one plan, once and for all, but *the conscious selection by the people of successive plans.* It was Whitman the democrat who warned that "the goal that was named cannot be countermanded."

If this conception of planning is sound, as I believe, then it is plain that in a democracy we always must rest our plans upon "here and now," upon "things as they are." How many are the bloody casualties of liberal efforts to improve the lot of man, how bitter the lost ground and disillusionment because of failure to understand so simple and yet so vital an issue of human strategy. So frequently have men sought an escape from the long task of education, the often prosaic day-by-day steps to "do something about it," by pressing for a plan—usually in the form of a law—without considering whether the people understand the reason for the law's plan, or how they are to benefit by it.

An unwillingness to start from where you are ranks as a fallacy of historic proportions; present-day planning, anywhere in the world for that matter, will fall into the same pit if it makes the same gigantic error. It is because the lesson of the past seems to me so clear on this score, because the nature of man so definitely confirms it, that there has been this perhaps tiresome repetition throughout this record: the people must be in on the planning; their existing institutions must be made part of it; self-education of the citizenry is more important than specific projects or physical changes.

And it is because of this same conviction that the TVA has never attempted by arbitrary action to "eliminate" or to force reform upon those factors or institutions in the valley's life which are vigorously antagonistic to a plan for unified development.

We move step by step—from where we are. Everyone has heard the story of the man who was asked by a stranger how he could get to Jonesville; after long thought and unsuccessful attempts to explain the several turns that must be made, he said, so the anecdote runs: "My friend, I tell you; if I were you, I wouldn't start from here." Some planning is just like that; it does not start from here; it assumes a "clean slate" that never has and never can exist.

The TVA idea of planning sees action and planning not as things separate and apart, but as one single and continuous process. In the President's message to the Congress in 1933, this fact was stressed. The words bear repetition here: The TVA, he said, "should be charged with the broadest duty of planning for the proper use, conservation, and development of the natural resources of the Tennessee River drainage basin and its adjoining territory for the general social and economic welfare of the Nation." Then follows this sentence: "This Authority should also be clothed with the necessary power to carry these plans into effect." And the law enacted this principle.

This is fundamental. And yet it is here that much of the disagreement with TVA has arisen from outside, and in its first years internal disagreement as well. The idea that planning and responsibility for action may and should be divorced—the maker of plans having little or nothing to do with their execution—follows the analogy of the planning of a house, an office building, any fixed structure. But the analogy is a mistaken one. For the development of a region is a course of action; it has no arbitrary point of beginning and goes on and on with no point of completion. The individual acts that make up regional development are the day-to-day activities of plowing a particular field, harvesting timber from a particular tract, the building of a factory, a church, a house, a highway. TVA's purpose was not the making of plans but that a valley be developed.

Plans had to be made, of course, many of them. But plans and action are part of one responsibility. TVA is responsible not alone for plans but for results. Those results depend chiefly upon the people's participation. Getting that participation was to be almost wholly on a voluntary basis. To get a job done in this way was a unique assignment, one that required the invention of new devices and new methods. If TVA had been a "planning agency" in the sense that its responsibility had been limited to the making of plans—the usual meaning of the term—those plans would probably have met the fate of so many other plans: brochures decorating bookshelves, adornments of the bibliography of a sterile learning.

In *The Coming Victory of Democracy*, Thomas Mann put his finger on this deep-lying error of intellectualism that treats planning apart from action. His words are moving, for they tell much of the causes beneath the catastrophe of European culture:

Democracy is thought; but it is thought related to life and action. . . . No intellectual of the pre-democratic era ever thought of action, nor of what kind of action would result if his thinking were put into practice. It is characteristic of undemocratic or of democratically uneducated nations that their thinking goes on without reference to reality, in pure abstraction, in complete isolation of the mind from life itself, and without the slightest consideration for the realistic consequences of thought.[2]

In the TVA the merging of planning and responsibility for the carrying out of those plans forces our technicians to make them a part of the main stream of living in the region or community; this it is that breathes into plans the breath of life. For in the Tennessee Valley the expert cannot escape from the consequences of his planning, as he can and usually does where it is divorced from execution. This has a profound effect on the experts themselves. Where planning is conceived of in this way, the necessity that experts should be close to the problems with which they are dealing is evident.

In my opinion the idea of planning is still struggling for popular support in America largely for this reason: that the most spectacular plans have been drawn by men who did not have the responsibility for carrying them out. They did not have the salutary discipline which the experts of this valley had who have had to ask themselves: "Is this a plan that I can take re-

[2] (New York: Alfred A. Knopf, Inc., 1939) p. 28.

sponsibility for seeing carried out? Will the people understand it, will the people help to make it effective? Will they make the plan their own?"

In the work of the TVA we have taken to heart and sought to put into practice what seems to me one of the most profound utterances upon the problem of freedom through democracy. They are the words of John Dewey.

The conflict as it concerns the democracy to which our history commits us [he wrote] is *within* our own institutions and attitudes. It can be won only by extending the application of democratic methods, methods of consultation, persuasion, negotiation, communication, co-operative intelligence, in the task of making our own politics, industry, education, our cultures generally, a servant and an evolving manifestation of democratic ideas. . . .

. . . democratic ends demand democratic methods for their realization . . . Our first defense is to realize that democracy can be served only by the slow day-by-day adoption and contagious diffusion in every phase of our common life of methods that are identical with the ends to be reached . . . An American democracy can serve the world only as it demonstrates in the conduct of its own life the efficacy of plural, partial, and experimental methods in securing and maintaining an ever-increasing release of the powers of human nature, in service of a freedom which is co-operative and a co-operation which is voluntary.[3]

What of the enforcement of economic and social plans in this valley? In the building of dams and other structures, TVA of course has the power which even private utilities and railroads have, to take property of landowners who are unwilling to sell, at a price fixed by court proceedings. But, beyond that, in no significant particular is TVA planning for the development of this region enforceable by law. And this we have not found to be a handicap.

This is not to say dogmatically that there is never any justification whatever for regulatory measures, or that voluntary methods have not resulted in a good many mistakes and

[3] *Freedom and Culture* (New York: G. P. Putnam's Sons, 1939), pp. 175-6.

waste that good planning would have avoided, if the people who made those decisions had been persuaded to make different ones. It is pointed out to us constantly that the course of education and voluntary action is too slow, that only the force of law will meet the crisis of depletion. Our critics, admitting that not a little progress has been made by our methods, point to the many farmers who still persist in plowing higher and higher on their hills, planting more corn and cotton, destroying more and more land; to the timber interests which continue to spurn the advice of forest technicians that would sustain the yield of lumber; to the manufacturers who still pollute the streams with waste and show scant interest in technical means of ending this contamination. More than once industries have been located at points where it seemed clear to us that sound planning should discourage industrial location.

This lack of power to enforce plans has disturbed a good many observers and students of the enterprise, especially in the early years, and still mystifies and even angers some of them. But we have continued to rely wholly upon the methods described in this book, the ways of contract, persuasion, incentives, encouragement, methods based on the people's confidence in TVA's comprehension, its good faith, and the quality of its technical leadership. I feel strongly that the admitted limitations of voluntary methods, distressing and tragic as their consequences sometimes are, do not invalidate the wisdom of a *minimum of coercion* in carrying out plans for resource development. For coercion is insatiable. In whatever guise, once coercion becomes the accepted reliance for making planning effective, more and more coercion is needed. I am deeply persuaded that high as the price of voluntary methods may be, in delays and errors, in the end the price of arbitrary enforcement of planning is nothing less than our freedom.

Chapter 19

TVA AND WORLD RECONSTRUCTION

AMONG the more than eleven million people who have visited the TVA in recent years have been representatives of almost every country in the world. Since the war there has been a marked increase in foreign visitors. They come in a steady procession: a Chinese general returning to Chungking, complete with military cape and battle dagger, an agricultural commissioner from New Delhi, the British Ambassador, a group of Swedish journalists especially observant of the modern architecture of the new powerhouses, a Brazilian scientist, a prominent Australian politician, a Czech electrical expert—hundreds of men from the most distant lands.

The TVA has also served as a training ground for foreign technicians; two score engineers and agriculturists from a dozen republics of South America; a similar contingent from China, singularly enthusiastic and intense. There has been a group of Russian engineers working with TVA technicians on Lend Lease hydro-electric plants that in 1944 will be producing power on streams "somewhere beyond the Urals."

This steady stream of "visiting" reminds you of the way in which a farmer crosses the ridge to take a look at a neighbor's demonstration farm, to see "how he does it," so he can try it out in his own way on his own place—except that these neighbors may be from Auckland on the other side of the globe, or from Göteborg, Buenos Aires, or Tegucigalpa. Among the visitors from abroad are not only policy-makers but experts in the many specialized fields embraced in this undertaking: from public health to mapping, from resettlement to community planning. Here they observe how their particular specialized interest can be made an integral part of the whole task of resource development.

This same world-wide interest is reflected in thousands of letters from many nations. The questions propounded, the material requested, the inquiries about how TVA proceeded, reflect a remarkable degree of interest in regional resource development. In recent months this correspondence has been largely from officials of post-war commissions of reconstruction, representatives of governments in exile, and legislators of Western Hemisphere nations. Writers in foreign magazines and newspapers describe TVA and set out what they believe are the lessons for their homeland in what is going on in this far-away and hitherto little known region. A leading English publication, *The Architectural Review*, for example, devoted its entire June, 1943, issue to a lengthy description and interpretation of TVA by Julian Huxley, the distinguished scientist and publicist. In a concluding paragraph he says:

Last, but not least, the TVA idea, of the planned development of natural regions such as river valleys, has already found its way into the world's general thinking. TVA ideas and methods are helping to guide the growth of new planning agencies such as the Middle East Supply Council; studies are being made of how a set-up of general TVA type could be adapted to serve as an international instead of a national agency (thus among other things undercutting and transcending nationalist sovereignties, as the TVA undercuts and transcends States' rights and boundaries), and adjusted to promote the planned development of regions of greater backwardness, like parts of Africa.

Our foreign visitors see with particular clarity that TVA speaks in a tongue that is universal, a language of *things close to the lives of people*: soil fertility, forests, electricity, phosphate, factories, minerals, rivers. No English interpreter is needed when a Chinese or a Peruvian sees this series of working dams, or electricity flowing into a simple farmhouse, or acres that phosphate has brought back to life. For it is not really Norris Dam on a Tennessee stream or a farm in Georgia that he sees, but a river, a valley, a farm in China or Peru. The changes that are taking place here are much the same as those which men all over the world are seeking. The technical problems, too, at bottom are essentially similar, whether one is dealing with soil erosion along the Yangtze or the Hiwassee, the malaria mosquito in Burma or Mississippi's Tishomingo County, power production in Norrland in Sweden or Swain County, North Carolina.

TVA's development of democratic methods of consent and participation by the people also touches a desire that is widely shared. Again and again our visitors have made substantially this comment: "We are even more interested in TVA's way of working with people than we are in its dams and furthering of industrial development." That resource development should not only be *for* the people of the valley but *by* them appeals to most of our foreign visitors. For like human beings almost everywhere they want to see the changes they hope to work out for their own countries done *in their own way*. This is important for Americans to remember, especially those who want to do the world over exactly on our own pattern, either on a cost-plus basis, or as a kind of paternalistic imperialism.

The TVA experience in resource development is being earnestly examined for the lessons it may hold for a battered world facing the giant contours of a historic period of reconstruction. For it is coming to be recognized ever more widely that our hope of future peace or the certainty of new wars rests to an important degree upon the wisdom the world can summon to the task of resource development. This is not the whole story of course; the effect of racial antagonisms and conflicting cultures on political systems goes deep. But at the root of much of the world's turbulence lies the way we deal with the physical base of every man's and hence every nation's livelihood.

The subject has the broadest ramifications; to pursue them is outside the scope of this book. It is obvious, however, that the pressure of people upon resources that do not adequately support them has long nourished a spirit of armed aggression against other nations. It is a commonplace that the development of one people's land and forests and minerals for the sole benefit of another people has started many a fire of hatred that later exploded into war. It has not, however, been quite so apparent that methods of unified development to create sustained productivity rather than quick exhaustion, that technical advance which makes low-grade ores, for example, as useful as the scarce higher grades, or that expert skills which can restore now wasted land and greatly increase its productivity, relieve war-creating tensions of impoverishment and may be the foundation stones upon which peace in a modern world can be slowly built. It is the light which this valley's experience throws on such matters— the brass tacks of world reconstruction—that has made it a center of interest to foreign visitors.

The TVA has come to be thought of (here and abroad) as a symbol of man's capacity to create and to build not only for war and death but for peace and life. This is of great importance in the post-war period. For despair and cynicism in our own ranks will be a deadly enemy after Germany and Japan surrender. The immediate task of fighting keeps us tense. Once that tension is relaxed we must be prepared for a let-down, a bitter loss of faith and hope. When that time comes it will be desperately important as a matter of mental antisepsis that there be, in this country and abroad, many living proofs, of which the TVA is one, of the creative powers of mankind and of democracy's demonstrated and practical concern for the everyday aspirations of people.

The value of TVA as a symbol of what man can do to change his physical environment is increased by the knowledge that in this valley we have had to face so many of those same problems which plague other regions of the world: low income, resignation to the *status quo* as "inevitable," complacency on the part of other more favored areas. A demonstration that such gains can be made without forcible changes in social status or property rights, without liquidating all those who do not agree completely with one's plans, will be evidence to support the conviction of those who have no faith in catastrophe as an instrument of human social improvement.

What I have said in the preceding chapter on "planning," on the importance of starting from where you are and of taking a step at a time, *one change promoting the next*, applies with peculiar force to our economic and political thinking about the post-war world. What is dumfounding to me, however, is that men who show they understand this as applied to our own affairs, when they consider the future of world society will abruptly slip these hawsers of experience and reality. They would be quick to condemn TVA if it had sought to make this valley over according to a pattern of TVA's own design. Yet they seem quite eager that America try the even more quixotic task of building a world order on the same kind of undemocratic foundation.

There is yet another way the TVA may throw the light of experience on the conditions for a lasting peace. For TVA is a demonstration, and one that can be readily understood, of this truth: *in any perspective of time, unified resource development anywhere helps everyone everywhere*. A stronger, more productive Tennessee Valley region has benefited the whole American nation and all its regions. So it will be when any region of the world strengthens the basis of its livelihood. Regional economic developments, whether within the nation or the family of nations, are not something to fear but to encourage.

When people of the more developed regions of the earth cease their fear that resource development and greater productiveness elsewhere injure them, and realize instead that they are benefited by them, then international political co-operation will be on the way to full realization. For it is that fear which nourishes extreme nationalism, with its harvest of hatred between peoples, tariff barriers, restrictive trade, autarchy, and finally—war. The physical shrinking of the world only multiplies the opportunities for inflaming these deep anxieties.

It is upon a wide popular comprehension and practice of the

economics of the Golden Rule—and particularly among our fellow Americans—that it seems to me the prospects for world peace largely rest. The essential structure of political co-operation between nations will be weakened, may indeed begin to crack the day it is set up, unless those political arrangements rest upon increasingly effective economic co-operation.

The experience of the Tennessee Valley helps to make these matters clearer to American public opinion, and thus serves a useful educational purpose in world reconstruction. It was a favorite argument against the TVA in its earliest years that the development of this valley would endanger the prosperity of the people elsewhere—in Ohio and Connecticut and New York. If an additional factory is built in Alabama—so the oft-repeated story ran—that will mean less factory employment in Ohio; if Tennessee produces more dairy products, that means a loss to the dairying industry in Wisconsin. Such ideas, seriously put forward in editorials and speeches about the TVA, rested upon the assumption that there is a market for just so much goods, and that America had now reached its highest level of production and of consumption.

Until the falseness of such ideas *within our own country* is understood at the grass roots, it is politically naïve to expect American public opinion to support the idea of encouraging world-wide economic co-operation in the interest of lasting peace. That many of us would prefer that such a policy be adopted primarily upon ethical grounds, and would favor it even if it hurt us economically, is quite irrelevant.

These things can be best understood by demonstrations that are close to us. Therein lies the value of TVA. For many people in Ohio, for example, or Connecticut, or New York, have come to see that increased productivity in the Tennessee Valley has not endangered their own standard of living as they were repeatedly told it would. The millions of people in this region who have been producing more, who thereby have been able to buy and enjoy more automobiles, radios, refrigerators, and clothes, make for a more prosperous nation and a stronger Ohio,

Connecticut, New York. The figures I have cited of increase in the level of income among the valley's people can be readily translated into the language of more production in *every* region.

Ten years ago the Tennessee Valley was regarded in the electrical appliance industry as the "zero" market of the country; a few years later it was the leading market of the entire country, with the spectacular increases in purchases that I have previously recited. The men in the General Electric shops at Schenectady, New York, or at the Westinghouse Company in Mansfield, Ohio, who produced many of those additional tens of thousands of electric ranges, water pumps, and refrigerators, now can see that it was in their interest that this valley had become productive enough to buy and pay for the products of their shops. This meant that men in Schenectady would buy overalls and aluminum goods made in this valley; could perhaps afford a fishing vacation on one of the new TVA lakes.

There was at the outset bitter opposition to the TVA from the coal industry, an opposition which further illustrates how mistaken it is to cling to the ideal of restricted development. The argument was made that by developing electricity from the water of the river TVA would rob the coal industry of its existing market for coal for steam-generated electricity. Actually, of course, sound development of one asset, water power, and a rate policy that increased its use enormously, inevitably stimulated the use of other resources, coal included. The valley market for coal for industrial and other purposes rose to heights never before experienced. Even the use of the region's coal for power generation has exceeded all records, as TVA's electric rate example multiplied power use over wide areas where coal is the principal source of electricity. Never has as much coal been used for the generation of electricity, as since the river has been developed. TVA itself has built and acquired steam-electric plants to supplement the river's power; in 1940 TVA purchased 574,000 tons of coal; in 1941, 693,000 tons; in 1942, 1,319,000 tons, chiefly for power production.

This is the way—by one object lesson after another—we

learn that the dangers to us of economic development elsewhere in the world are imaginary. When Americans see that it has helped, not hurt, the people of Ohio, say, to have this southern valley more productive, we shall see that much the same thing will be true if, in their own way, Mexicans and Brazilians and Russians and Chinese develop their resources and trade with us and with each other. That comprehension can best be learned at first hand.

It is folly to expect Americans clearly to see the tragedy, *for the world,* of an intense nationalism until restrictive section-alism *within the nation* is also seen as a self-defeating policy. A demand for an end of a colonial system far from home is not nearly so important as an understanding of the colonial system within the United States, and the reasons why it is so injurious to this nation's interest. And colonialism, or exploiting the hinter-land, is substantially the basis upon which the South and the West have been so long predominantly a raw-materials source for the dominant manufacturing regions of the North and Northeast.

American public opinion on world co-operation will not be strengthened by the kind of double talk that displays fervid concern for self-development for India along with lack of interest, even hostility, toward industrial development for undeveloped American regions. Such a cynical attitude will justify the sus-picion that far-off China's cause is espoused and that of near-by Georgia and Arkansas ignored because there are fewer Amer-ican vested interests—political and economic—to be antag-onized. Equality of opportunity for all the nations of the world will yield few benefits to the average man if that great principle is dissociated from specific issues of equality of opportunity for regions within our own country.

World co-operation cannot be built on mere expansiveness of spirit, or upon escapes from the reality of hard work close at hand. It is in our own backyard that we can best prove the sincerity of our aims for the wide world, and best learn the great truth of universal interdependence. In the teaching of this truth, by action and not words alone, TVA has a limited but useful role.

We have still a long way to go in public understanding of these matters. As recently as the spring of 1943 the Governor of one of our great eastern industrial states, a man of national leadership, warned against the growth of industry in the South and West upon the ground that it would injure his state, apparently on the assumption that greater industrial activity here inevitably meant net losses to his state. His remarks were occasioned in part by a series of TVA reports to Congress. In these reports we urged, in the national interest, the end of a system of regional freight rates that are much higher in the South and West than in the industrial North and East. We recommended a national rate without discrimination against any region.

With freight rates on goods manufactured in the South almost 40 per cent higher, mile for mile, than on goods manufactured north of the Ohio (though railroad unit costs are almost identical), a manufacturer to establish himself in the South and in other similarly disadvantaged regions must carry a heavy handicap. No wonder progress in southern industry has been so slow and difficult, and the pressure to pay low wages so great. Moreover, since it is manufacture that gives opportunity for those skills which yield the highest returns, income in the American colonial regions is far below that of the industrial regions of the North. It was inevitable that with this disadvantage against manufacture, the South and West have had to drain their natural resources of soil fertility, timber, minerals, and oil, unwisely and often disastrously. By contrast, favorable freight rates on raw materials encouraged this exploitation.

The elimination of this man-made handicap of regional rates, TVA believes, would enable the South and West to increase the amount of manufacturing of their raw materials, since then the internal tariff walls of freight rates would no longer bar their manufactured goods from free movement to their economic markets. The people's income would accordingly rise, for low income and reliance upon raw materials are the marks the world over of the colonial system.

TVA has insisted that this change would not rob Peter in the North to swell the lean pockets of Paul in the interior, but would *benefit both regions*. And here precisely is the importance of the freight rate issue in the development of an American public opinion favorable to world economic co-operation. It must become clear to Americans generally that the increased productiveness of the undeveloped regions of this country is to the advantage of the whole country and all of its regions. Otherwise it is a forlorn hope to believe that the equivalent principle in world affairs will receive effective and continuous American popular support.

To what extent and under what terms should private investors or the government of this country finance the development of resources in other parts of the world as a means of buttressing the pillars of peace? A complete discussion of this is obviously beyond the scope of this book. The point I seek to make is simply this: the issue ought not be thought of in terms of fear of "creating competition against our own businessmen and farmers." This fear has as little general validity in the international field as it has between regions here at home. The policy of reciprocal trade, for example, takes on meaning only when there is trade, i.e., productiveness, to reciprocate. The flourishing regions and nations can only *remain* vigorous and strong by encouraging the regions and nations that are less productive.

Whether we encourage or discourage it, or are foolish enough to regard it with indiscriminate fear, world-wide development of natural resources and industrialization will go forward rapidly after the war. The United States can in some ways speed the process and influence its course. But it is nonsense to believe that we hold a broad veto over what other great nations decide to do in developing their rivers or their other resources. To accept such shallow talk as this is to close our eyes to the central fact that sets our time off from all that went before—the drive, the world over, toward resource development through the machine and science.

There are, however, questions that are still open: what *course* the development will take, both here and abroad; the *methods* that will be used; for whose *benefit* the development will be carried out. Unless the people demand a course that will benefit them, one that will not exhaust their resources wastefully, the old exploitative methods of the elite few are likely to be followed.

It is for this reason that the TVA experience ought to be known. For a knowledge of the methods followed in this valley's development will enable the people to be critical, to demand answers to their questions—questions such as these: Will economic development be unified, seen as a whole? Will resources be regarded as a means of benefiting the human beings who depend upon them, or will the development of each resource be deemed as an end in itself, its benefits drained off by a few with no recognition of broad ethical purpose? Will resource development be treated as merely a physical task for technicians and businessmen; or will it be seen to be a democratic opportunity as well, the essence of which is the participation of the people, the acceptance of their evolving ideas of what is good, of what it is they want?

Will these new projects be administered by the methods of remote control and extreme centralization, invitations to tyranny; or will decentralized administration of central policies be the general principle? Will these developments be energized and directed by modern tools for getting things done; or by archaic methods of administration, crusted with tradition and fortified by bureaucratic "rights"? Unless the decisions are to go by default to those who always watch out for their own selfish interests, these are some of the questions that should be faced by the people, in our country and in others, as the time draws ever closer when action can take the place of plans for post-war development.

The use abroad of the public corporation as a tool to accomplish resource development after the war, in both mature and undeveloped regions, has been the object of extensive discussion. In other countries there has been much the same reaction as in the United States against the traditional bureau as an instrument to accomplish modern needs. There is a growing recognition that the autonomous corporation can get certain kinds of things done that other more customary government agencies somehow do not. In other countries, too, it has apparently been almost impossible in any other way to secure the adoption of modern management methods in government. Whether in Britain, China, or Australia, there appears to a remarkable degree the same need to cut away from the ritualism of traditional agencies' methods. The public corporation appears to be one of the ways of achieving this purpose. The TVA's adoption of business methods and management devices has accordingly been the subject of considerable firsthand study by foreign observers.

The public development corporation, following the broad lines of the TVA, is also a possible medium for administering *international* resource projects, i.e., the development of resources lying in more than one country, in which control and responsibility must be divided between several nations or their citizens. This has been given a good deal of consideration, particularly in Great Britain, in discussions of the development of Central Europe—the Danube River Valley, for example. Various forms of international development corporations have been proposed. "Such an international public corporation," writes Mr. Lewis L. Lorwin, "may prove as useful a device for opening up international economic activity in the twentieth century as did the private corporation in the nineteenth century." He concludes that the public corporation, based upon "its proved value on the national level, as demonstrated by the Tennessee Valley Authority in the United States and by the British Broadcasting Corporation in England . . . offers, in the international field . . . an opportunity to achieve social purposes, under public control, by business operations with a maximum of flexibility and a minimum of restraint by standardized bureaucratic procedures."[1]

But the use of the public corporation, in itself (while it might be very useful), would have only an incidental relation to the TVA idea unless it were the instrument of the basic idea of unified development within a natural region.

Whether a river is wholly within a single nation or flows through several countries does not affect the technical problems of its development or the necessity of dealing with it as a unity. A river has no nationality. The Danube River, for example, is oblivious of the national animosities or the many boundary lines along its course from the Black Forest through Bavaria, Austria, Hungary, Yugoslavia, Bulgaria, and Rumania, until its three mouths pour its water into the Black Sea. The sound of its name changes as it flows along—Donau, Dunau, Dunav, Dunarea— but the river itself is as little affected by political differences as by the different names by which it is known. Such a river valley has a unity that is of nature; its development in accordance with this oneness would require an international agency; the TVA public-private prototype might be the best available.

These are interesting speculations, but they must not be taken to prove too much. The differences between the people in such a natural region, their ancient disunity, racial antagonisms, barriers of custom and language, are as real in human affairs as they are unreal to a river or a forest. The common development by all these peoples of a single river may serve to ease these old tensions. But it would be tragic, by any oversimple analogies between nature and men's institutions, to underestimate the difficulties.

A final word about the place of the TVA idea in the development of world economic co-operation. Resource development in the United States in accordance with the principle of unity can mean a period of expanding industry and agriculture. It can mean more income, more jobs, adventures in new enterprise for trained brains and hands. Contrariwise, if we neglect or ignore the signs of resource exhaustion, and if we persist in

[1] "New Frontiers Abroad," *Survey Graphic*, May, 1943, p. 212.

wasteful use of what nature has provided for us, we increase the hazard of contraction, retrenchment, "hanging on to what we have," and the fears and uneasiness which that kind of stability creates. Such a climate of caution and scarcity will increase greatly the political difficulties of American participation in world affairs. It may even make them impossible. Workmen without jobs or afraid they may soon be, businessmen harassed by the problems of retrenchment and failing markets, farmers worried about raising crops without any assurance that city people will have the money to buy them—these are not people who are in a mood to co-operate with other nations.

What American public opinion will support in world affairs may well depend upon whether at the hour of decision the dominant feeling at home is optimism and good will, or the fearful grasping of worried men intent on "saving their own necks" by letting the world go hang. Such an escape is only an illusion, but frightened men will embrace it. In all but the best-disciplined spirits panic kills the natural, warmhearted impulse to work with one's neighbors. An expanding prosperous nation is not necessarily one that is willing to take its share of world responsibilities; but we can be sure that never will a frightened nation play a great role in world affairs.

In the Tennessee Valley this development has created an expansive spirit, a note of confidence and hope in the future. To the extent that resource development in America after the war can aid in this way to stimulate confidence among businessmen, farmers, and workers, it may have important spiritual consequences that go beyond the bare bones of economics. It may thereby improve the chances of creating and maintaining an American public opinion upon which may rest the world's hopes for peace.

Chapter 20

IT CAN BE DONE: DREAMERS WITH SHOVELS

IN THIS one of the thousand valleys of the earth the physical setting of men's living has improved. Each day the change becomes more pronounced. The river is productive, the land more secure and fruitful, the forests are returning, factories and workshops and new houses and electric lines have put a different face upon the Tennessee Valley.

Is this really genuine improvement? Has it enhanced the quality of human existence? Are men's lives richer, fuller, more "human" as a result of such changes in our physical surroundings? To most people, I am sure, the answer is in the clear affirmative. But, in appraising the meaning of this valley's experience, the doubts on this score can by no means be ignored, nor dealt with out of hand; people not only raise such questions but answer them differently from the way most of us would answer them.

There are those who believe that material progress does not and cannot produce good, and may indeed stand as a barrier to it. To those, and there are many who hold such belief, mechanical progress, technology, the machine, far from improving the lot of men are actually seen as a source of debasement and condemned as "materialism."

The whole theme and thesis of this book challenges these ideas and the philosophy upon which they rest. I do not, of course, believe that when men change their physical environment they are inevitably happier or better. The machine that frees a man's back of drudgery does not thereby make his spirit free. Technology has made us more productive, but it does not necessarily enrich our lives. Engineers can build us great dams, but only great people make a valley great. There is no technology of goodness. Men must make themselves spiritually free.

But because these changes in our physical environment in the valley do not in and of themselves make us happier, more generous, kinder, it does not follow that they have no relation to our spiritual life.

We have a choice. There is the important fact. Men are not powerless; they have it in their hands to use the machine to augment the dignity of human existence. True, they may have so long denied themselves the use of that power to decide, which is theirs, may so long have meekly accepted the dictation of bosses of one stripe or another or the ministrations of benevolent nursemaids, that the muscles of democratic choice have atrophied. But that strength is always latent; history has shown how quickly it revives. How we shall *use* physical betterment —that decision is ours to make. We are not carried irresistibly by forces beyond our control, whether they are given some mystic term or described as the "laws of economics." We are not inert objects on a wave of the future.

Except for saints and great ascetics, I suppose most people would agree that poverty and physical wretchedness are evils, in and of themselves. But because extreme poverty is an evil it does not follow that a comfortable or a high material standard of living is good. A Tennessee Valley farm wife who now has an electric pump that brings water into her kitchen may or may not be more generous of spirit, less selfish, than when she was forced to carry her water from the spring day after day. A once destitute sharecropper who now has an interesting factory job at good wages and lives in a comfortable house in town may or may not be more tolerant, more rational, more thoughtful of others, more active in community concerns. We all know that some of the least admirable men are found among those who have come up from poverty to a "high standard of living."

Whether happiness or unhappiness, freedom or slavery, in

short whether good or evil results from an improved environment depends largely upon how the change has been brought about, upon the methods by which the physical results have been reached, and in what spirit and for what purpose the fruits of that change are used. Because a higher standard of living, a greater productiveness and a command over nature are not good in and of themselves does not mean that we cannot make good of them, that they cannot be a source of inner strength.

The basic objection to all efforts to use the machine for human betterment lies in an attitude of absolute pessimism: that life is an evil in itself; that therefore anything which seeks to mitigate its inescapable pain and utter dullness is misdirected and futile. To men who in sincerity and passion hold to this faith, there is no answer that will satisfy them. Although there are few people in America who would admit that they hold such sweepingly negative views, they are nevertheless important; for such a faith (or lack of faith) colors and affects far less drastic but far more widely held objections to material changes. Many people, for example, although not denying the worth of life itself, are committed to the closely related belief that mankind is essentially wicked and naturally and irretrievably inclined to evil. This "prodigious malignity of the human heart," they assert, marks down as folly and misguided any efforts to improve men's physical surroundings.

That there are evil tendencies in mankind few who have lived through the last quarter century would care to deny. But of this I am sure and confident: the *balance*, the overwhelming balance, is on the side of good. This is a matter of faith, for where is the statistician or logician who can prove or disprove on which side the balance stands? But by the very act of faith in the essential goodness of men we further that goodness, just as the Nazi faith in the wickedness of men has nourished human animality and depravity by the very act of believing in it.

Democracy is a literal impossibility without faith that on balance the good in men far outweighs the evil. Every effort to cherish the overtones of human imagination in music, painting, or poetry rests upon that same faith, makes that same assumption. And so it is with what we have been seeking to do in this valley. To call it "materialistic" answers nothing. The rock upon which all these efforts rest is a faith in human beings.

I recognize that I am dealing with a broad issue of religious and philosophical thought upon which a great debate has raged for centuries and still continues. But it cannot be ignored, even if it cannot here be adequately discussed. I must let the matter rest, for present purposes, by quoting the statements of two modern thinkers upon this matter, whose words state the essentials of my own conviction.

The first is that of the great contemporary philosopher of China, Dr. Hu Shih, until recently Ambassador to the United States. He refers to the argument embraced as truth by countless millions in the Orient, and by not a few among our own people, that improvements in physical surroundings are no aid to the spirit, and that those civilizations which regard such advances as important are "materialistic." Then he says:

> For to me that civilization is materialistic which is limited by matter and incapable of transcending it; which feels itself powerless against its material environment and fails to make the full use of human intelligence for the conquest of nature and for the improvement of the conditions of man. Its sages and saints may do all they can to glorify contentment and hypnotize the people into a willingness to praise their gods and abide by their fate. But that very self-hypnotizing philosophy is more materialistic than the dirty houses they live in, the scanty food they eat, and the clay and wood with which they make the images of their gods.
>
> On the other hand, that civilization which makes the fullest possible use of human ingenuity and intelligence in search of truth in order to control nature and transform matter for the service of mankind, to liberate the human spirit from ignorance, superstition, and slavery to the forces of nature, and to reform social and political institutions for the benefit of the greatest number—such a civilization is highly idealistic and spiritual.[1]

[1] *Whither Mankind*, ed. Beard (New York: Longmans, Green and Co., 1937) pp. 40-1.

The words of Pope Pius XI, in his famous encyclical *Quadragesimo Anno*, are equally simple, and the conclusion he draws convincing:

Then only will the economic and social organism be soundly established and attain its end, when it secures for all and each those goods which the wealth and resources of nature, technical achievement and the social organization of economic affairs can give. These goods should be sufficient to supply all needs and an honest livelihood, and to uplift men to that higher level of prosperity and culture which, provided it be used with prudence, is not only no hindrance but is of singular help to virtue.

But in addition to the philosophical protests there is a further and more widely held objection to such an enterprise as we have seen in this valley. The hideous belief has been spread over the earth that the price of material progress and freedom from want must be the complete surrender of individual freedom. The acceptance of this doctrine has been indeed the principal event of our lifetime. And it remains the faith of the people of Germany and Japan, the most advanced technical nations on the continent of Europe and in all the Orient.

Here in the United States, too, there are people of great influence who have essentially that conviction. They seek to persuade America, chiefly by subtle indirection, that modern technology demands that ordinary people (they do not, of course, think of themselves as such) abandon the ideal of individual freedom and the right to a voice in their own destiny, that only by yielding up such mistaken ideas is it possible for modern industry to raise their "standard of living." There is irony and yet an awful fitness in the fact that arch-conservatives and ultra-radicals are joined in agreement at this point. This spirit of defeatism about the individual in modern life and therefore about democracy is far too widespread to be ignored, and the support it receives in our own country too great to be dismissed lightly.

The technical results in the Tennessee Valley, the achievements of many kinds of experts, are of course matters of no little importance. But, speaking as an administrator and a citizen, unless these technical products strengthen the conviction that machines and science can be used by men for their greater individual and spiritual growth, then so far as I am concerned the physical accomplishments and the material benefits would be of dubious value indeed.

There are few who fail to see that modern applied science and the machine are threats to the development of the individual personality, the very purpose of democratic institutions. It is for this reason that the experience of the last ten years in the valley of the Tennessee is heartening. In this one valley (in some ways the world in microcosm) it has been demonstrated that methods can be developed—methods I have described as grass-roots democracy—which do create an opportunity for greater happiness and deeper experience, for freedom, in the very course of technical progress. Indeed this valley, even in the brief span of a decade, supports a conviction that when the use of technology has a moral purpose and when its methods are thoroughly democratic, far from forcing the surrender of individual freedom and the things of the spirit to the machine, the machine can be made to promote those very ends.

It is enormously important that we have that conviction, that we have evidence which clearly supports that conviction. For here is the reality: This job must be done, this task of changing our physical environment through science and the machine. It ought to be done by democrats, by those who believe that people come first, by those who have faith in the capacities of many men and not of only a few. It cannot be done by defeatists. And it ought not be done by those who believe that human beings are inherently wicked. But it is a job that must be done. And it will be done—*by someone.* The only questions open are: How will it be done? Who will benefit? The answers will largely be provided by that intangible known as faith.

Faith is the greatest power in the world of men, the most "practical" force of all. How is faith sustained and built ever stronger? By the redemption of faith through works. Take the simple case of a farmer on one of these demonstration farms. When you talk with him you can sense at once that his faith has been stirred. He has actually seen something happen on his own homestead that he never believed could come true for him. He has seen what science can do for his land, what it can do under his own rooftree, what it can do in his community among his neighbors. What he and his wife have seen with their eyes gives them added faith that other equally impossible things can happen, too, on their farm, in their community, in the nation. They come to feel—"It *can* be done."

Faith that individual personality can flourish side by side with the machine and with science is vital in this: that men have only to have a faith that is deep enough, a belief sufficiently firm, in their daily work and living, that these things can be done—and then they will be done. For no insoluble physical problems stand in the way. There is no insuperable material barrier. The only serious obstacles are in the minds of men. These are not inconsiderable, it is true, but thinking put them there; a new kind of thinking can remove them. The great thing that has transpired in the Tennessee Valley is this growing faith not only that the scientific progress of our time can be used as a tool to create higher income and more comfortable living, but that technology can give men a choice, a genuine choice of alternatives, and that it can be used to make men free as they have never been before.

But there must be more than a conviction, a sure confidence, that it can be done. There must be a *sense of urgency*, a sense that this is the day on which to turn the first shovel. There are some who dream great dreams but never feel this urgency "to do something about it." This is in character for the intellectual gone to seed, the perfectionist, the "cooler head," the defeatist, the nostalgic liberal, the cynic about human possibilities. They are preoccupied in conjuring up all the possible difficulties and multiplying them. But the dreamers with shovels in their hands know that to start is important. The dreamers with shovels want only a job that is magnificent enough, room enough to stand in, and a chance to make a start.

They see a start as only that. For this is a continuing process, this improving the physical environment of men. It is never finished. There is no end, no blueprint of a finished product.

I share with many of my neighbors in the Tennessee Valley a deep conviction that it can be done, the modern job of building our resources and making the machine work for all men. And because of our experience together we believe that it can be done by such methods and with such purposes as will enrich the things of the spirit. This experience convinces me that science and invention can be consciously and deliberately directed to achieving the kind of world that people want. If it is decentralized industry men want, "family farming," or pleasant cities not too large, an end to smoke and congestion and filth— there are modern tools which can be turned to just such ends. The people, working through their private enterprises and public institutions which are democratic in spirit, can get substantially the kind of community and country they want.

The physical job will be done. If not democratically, it will be done in an anti-democratic way. It will be done perhaps by a small group of huge private corporations, controlling the country's resources; or by a tight clique of politicians; or by some other group or alliance of groups that is ready to take this responsibility which the people themselves decline to take. The smooth-talking centralizers, the managerial elite, cynical politicians, everyone without faith in the capacities of the people themselves to find a way will be hard at work seeking to draw off the benefits and control the development of the resources by which in turn they will control the lives of men. These are the gravest of dangers. No one can minimize the hazards of the gathering storm, or fail to see that troubled days lie ahead for democracy in our country. But catastrophe need not befall us. If as a people, in our daily living, we will only use the strength our democratic inheritance gives us, these attacks from within can be turned back and decisively defeated. Democracy can emerge revitalized by the test and conflict.

Here in the valley where I have been writing this statement of faith, the people know the job of our time can be done, for they have read the signs and reaped the first token harvest. They know it can be done, not only *for* the people but *by* the people.

APPENDIX

SOME REFERENCES FOR TECHNICIANS

This is not a comprehensive bibliography on the Tennessee Valley Authority. The titles listed here are highly selective and with few exceptions, specialized in content to enable the professional or technical reader to get more particularized information about the TVA than this book presumes to give.

Many of the titles listed contain specialized bibliographies and were selected in part for that reason. A complete bibliography of books and periodical articles about the TVA would include more than 3500 titles. *The Agricultural Index, Industrial Arts Index, Engineering Index, Readers' Guide to Periodical Literature, Public Affairs Information Service Bulletin,* and *Education Index,* available in many public and educational libraries, will aid the reader in making his own reading list or in exploring any of the special phases of the TVA program. For important newspaper articles consult the *New York Times Index.*

The following indexes prepared by the TVA Technical Library and available in many libraries will give the reader additional references to the TVA program: (1) *Indexed Bibliography of the Tennessee Valley Authority,* (2) *Selected List of Books, Theses, and Pamphlets on TVA,* (3) *Congressional Hearings, Reports, and Documents Relating to TVA.*

This selected list of references was prepared by Bernard L. Foy, TVA Technical Librarian.

AGRICULTURE

Ball, Carleton R. *A Study of the Work of the Land-Grant Colleges in the Tennessee Valley Area in Cooperation with the Tennessee Valley Authority.* Knoxville, Tennessee: TVA, 1939. 76p.

Southwest Virginia Agricultural Association. *Building a New Dominion*. Knoxville, Tennessee: TVA, 1943. 34p.

An illustrated account of the activities and results of the Southwest Virginia Agricultural Association, undertaken in co-operation with the Agricultural Extension Division of the Virginia Polytechnic Institute and the TVA.

Community Refrigeration

Georgia. University. Division of Vocational Education. *Establishing a Community Refrigeration Service*. Athens, Georgia, June 1941. 31p. bibliog. mimeo. (Vocational Education in Agriculture, Vol. 23, No. 4).

Practical techniques for arousing interest in community refrigeration, with follow-through pointers on the building and financing of the plant itself.

Dehydration of Food

Georgia. State Board of Vocational Education. *Constructing a Community Food Dehydrator*. Atlanta, Georgia, March 1943. 15p. processed. (Special Bulletin No. 9).

Complete construction details, drawings, and estimated cost for building a 50 bushel size cabinet-type dehydrator.

Shuey, Guy A. *Dehydration of Fruits and Vegetables in the Home*. Knoxville, Tennessee, May 1943. 23p. bibliog. (Tennessee. University. Agricultural Experiment Station. Bulletin No. 183).

Selection and preparation of food for dehydrating, construction and operation of the home dehydrator, and packaging and refreshing the dried product.

Erosion Control

Tennessee Valley Authority. Department of Forestry Relations. *Manual for Soil Erosion Control in the Tennessee Valley—Engineering Phase*, by J. H. Nicholson and J. E. Snyder. Knoxville, Tennessee: TVA, October 15, 1939. 128p. processed.

The engineering aspects of erosion: its cause, recommendations and specifications for its control under varying conditions.

—— *Manual for Soil Erosion Control in the Tennessee Valley—Reforestation Phase*, by Richard Kilbourne and G. H. Lentz. Knoxville, Tennessee: TVA, October 1936. 57p. mimeo.

The establishment of a forest cover through reforestation is the second step in the control and reforestation of an eroded area.

Hay Drying Equipment

Weaver, John W., Jr. and Wylie, C. E. *Drying Hay in the Barn and Testing Its Feeding Value.* Knoxville, Tennessee, August 1939. 24p. bibliog. (Tennessee. University. Agricultural Experiment Station. Bulletin No. 170).

A history of experimentation in hay drying, and a description of the equipment necessary to barn-dry hay by forcing air through partially dried hay with an automatically controlled electric blower.

Phosphates and Farming

Tennessee. University. Agricultural Extension Service. *Farming for Victory and Peace; Some Lessons from Tennessee Unit Test Demonstration Farms.* Knoxville, Tennessee, June 1942. 14p. (Publication 263).

Examples of the value of phosphate fertilizer as seen on seven typical Tennessee farms.

Quick Freezing of Fruits and Vegetables

Ferris, John P. and Taylor, R. B. Immersion Quick Freezing, Its Application to Rural Processing Industry. bibliog. *Mechanical Engineering,* 61:437-442, June 1939.

The economic background for the freezing of perishable farm crops, and details of the freezing process experimentation, particularly with strawberries.

Rural Electrification Equipment

Beanblossom, F. Z. and Hunter, F. M. *Brood Healthy Chicks with Electricity.* State College, Mississippi, May 1940. 24p. (Mississippi. State College. Extension Service. Extension Bulletin No. 111).

The selection, construction, wiring and operation of an electric brooder house.

Tennessee. University. Agricultural Extension Service. *Household Equipment; Its Care and Simple Repair.* Knoxville, Tennessee, June 1943. 36p. (Publication 273).

Practical, illustrated instructions for the maintenance and protection of refrigerators, ranges, washing machines and other home appliances.

ARCHEOLOGY

Webb, William S. and DeJarnette, D. L. *An Archeological Survey of Pickwick Basin in the Adjacent Portions of the States of Alabama, Mississippi and Tennessee.* Washington: Government Printing Office, 1942. 536p. bibliog. (Smithsonian Institution. Bureau of American Ethnology. Bulletin 129).

Detailed report on the prehistory of the TVA Pickwick basin. Similar surveys have been made of the Norris and Wilson areas.

ARCHITECTURE

Tennessee Valley Authority Architecture as Published in the Magazine Pencil Points; Reprinted from *Pencil Points,* November 1939. Knoxville, Tennessee: TVA, 1940. 55p.

Articles and photographs which give an idea of the TVA architecture, its functional and aesthetic qualities.

TVA Architecture as Shown at the Museum of Modern Art; Reprinted from the *Magazine of Art,* 1938, 1940, 1941. Knoxville, Tennessee: TVA, 1941. 28p.

Excellent photographs of TVA architecture with brief descriptions.

Wank, Roland A. Architecture in Rural Areas—a Report on TVA Experience. *New Pencil Points,* 23:47-53, December 1942.

TVA's influence on the rural architecture of the valley, brought about by planning with townspeople and architects, and through exemplary buildings designed by TVA for its employees.

CHEMICAL ENGINEERING RESEARCH

Tennessee Valley Authority. Department of Chemical Engineering. *General Outline of Chemical Engineering Activities,* by Harry A. Curtis. Wilson Dam, Alabama: TVA, 1942. 44p. bibliog. (Chemical Engineering Report No. 1).

A broad outline of the TVA chemical engineering activities with a description of the major projects undertaken.

Electric Furnaces

Curtis, Harry A., Miller, A. M. and Junkins, J. N. A Collection of Articles on the Production of Superphosphate by the Electric Furnace Method. Reprinted from *Chemical & Metallurgical Engineering*, June, September 1935, August, November, December 1936.

A detailed discussion with diagrams of the electric furnace method of producing superphosphate. The problems involved, the records maintained, and the comparative costs of this furnace method are given.

Phosphates

U. S. Congress. Joint Committee to Investigate the Adequacy and Use of Phosphate Resources. *Phosphate Resources of the United States. Hearings . . . 75th Congress.* Washington: Government Printing Office, 1939. 1182p.

This Congressional hearing contains the testimony of several TVA officials regarding the adequacy and use of phosphate resources.

ELECTRICITY UTILIZATION

Munger, George D., Towne, C. A. and Voltz, P. W. Education in the Adaptation of the Valley People to New Factors in the Environment. *Journal of Educational Sociology*, 15:174-184, November 1941.

An outline of the educational programs employed to assist the people of the area in using the new electrical and recreational facilities around them, principally through demonstration techniques.

Power Sales

Tennessee Valley Authority. Department of Power Utilization. *Electricity Sales Statistics, Monthly Report No. 1-Date.* Chattanooga, Tennessee: TVA. processed.

Rates

Krug, J. A. Testimony on the TVA Power Program (In U. S. Congress. Joint Committee on the Investigation of the Tennessee Valley Authority. *Hearings . . . 75th Congress*. Washington: Government Printing Office, 1939. pt. 12, p. 5189-5203, 5227-5451, 5495-5509).

Rural Electrification

Morgan, Harcourt A. Rural Electrification; a Promise to American Life (In World Power Conference. 3d, Washington, D. C., 1936. *Transactions*, 8:769-799. Washington: Government Printing Office, 1938).

The problems of agriculture, population distribution, over-specialization, soil erosion, fluctuating prices and production, tenancy, and general decline are outlined, with the specific assistance which rural electrification can give to each problem.

ENGINEERING

Ransmeier, Joseph S. *The Tennessee Valley Authority; a Case Study in the Economics of Multiple Purpose Stream Planning*. Nashville, Tennessee: Vanderbilt University Press, 1942. 486p.

This book first seeks to set out the nature and objectives of the TVA by carefully reviewing the facts of its program and by analyzing the philosophy which governs its decisions. Secondly, it attempts, in a separate part, an analysis of joint cost apportionment.

Tennessee Valley Authority. *Report to the Congress on the Unified Development of the Tennessee River System*. Knoxville, Tennessee: TVA, March 1936. 105p.

Recommendations of the Board of Directors to Congress as to planning, general operating policies to be pursued, and a description of specific recommended projects.

Carrier-Current Control

Merritt, M. Stephens and Talmage, T. D. Carrier-Current Relaying and Communication on the TVA System. *Electrical Engineering*, 61:561-572, November 1942.

This article gives reasons for the selection of carrier relaying and communication and presents an analysis of their application, of the difficulties encountered, and of their over-all performance under service conditions.

Construction

Engineering News-Record. The Tennessee Valley Experiment; Reprinted from *Engineering News-Record*, December 3, 10, 17, 24, 31, 1936. 30p.

The background of TVA, and what has been attempted, accomplished, and anticipated in the fields of water conservation, flood control, navigation, power, and regional planning.

Cost Allocation

Tennessee Valley Authority. *Report on Investment in Wilson, Norris, Wheeler, Pickwick Landing, Guntersville, Chickamauga, Hiwassee, Nottely, Watts Bar Hydro, Watts Bar Steam, Chatuge And Cherokee Projects, and the Allocation of the Investment, Under Section 14, of the Tennessee Valley Authority Act, to the Several Purposes Served, and Notes on the Allocation, as of June 30, 1942.* Approved by the President February 1, 1943. Knoxville, Tennessee: TVA, 1943. 12p. mimeo.

Design

Rich, George R. and others. Design of Recent TVA Projects. *Civil Engineering*, 13:144-147, 165-167, 205-208, 257-260, 305-308, 373-376, 413-416, 465-468, March-October 1943.

A series of articles on the basic engineering design features of recent TVA power developments at Watts Bar, Fort Loudoun, Kentucky, Fontana, Cherokee, Douglas, Chatuge, Nottely, Apalachia and Ocoee No. 3.

Electrical Design

Hopkins, Raymond A. Tennessee Valley Authority Hydroelectric Stations—Electrical Design. *Electrical Engineering (Supplement, Transactions Section)*, 60:1281-1293, December 1941.

Discussion of the principal electrical design features of the ten hydroelectric stations designed and constructed or under construction by the TVA.

Flood Control

Tennessee Valley Authority. *Value of Flood Height Reduction from Tennessee Valley Authority Reservoirs to the Alluvial Valley of the Lower Mississippi River.* Washington: Government Printing Office, 1939. 64p. (76th Cong. H. Doc. 455).

Mapping

Talley, Benjamin B. *Engineering Applications of Serial and Terrestrial Photogrammetry.* New York: Pitman Publishing Corporation, 1938. p. 566-595.

Illustrates the uses of maps and aerial photographs, including TVA's use for rural rehabilitation.

Power Transmission

Woodruff, W. Warren and others. Power Transmission (In the *Standard Handbook for Electrical Engineers.* 7th ed. New York: McGraw-Hill Book Company, 1941. p. 1156-1312).

A technical discussion, with accompanying tables and formulae, on the design, construction and maintenance of power line systems, together with the economics involved.

Project Completion Reports

Tennessee Valley Authority. *The Norris Project.* Washington: Government Printing Office, 1940. 840p. bibliog. (Technical Report No. 1).

Detailed technical study, covering original project investigation, dam and powerhouse design and construction, transportation to the project, employee housing, and cost data. Similar studies have been prepared on the Wheeler, Pickwick Landing, Guntersville, and Chickamauga Projects.

FINANCIAL OPERATIONS

Mansfield, Harvey C. The Case of the TVA (In his *The Comptroller General.* New Haven, Connecticut: Yale University Press, 1939. p. 232-244).

A review of the relations of the TVA with the General Accounting Office as an illustration of the issues that arise between an administrative agency and the Comptroller General.

Tennessee Valley Authority. Comptroller. *Financial Statements for the Fiscal Years ending June 30, 1938-Date.* Knoxville, Tennessee: TVA. processed.

Gives balance sheet, operating statements for the main programs, and detailed schedules for dams and plants. Also available in TVA *Annual Reports.*

Tennessee Valley Authority. Comptroller. *Municipalities (Electric Departments Only) & Cooperatives, Purchasing Power from Tennessee Valley Authority. Financial Statements for the Fiscal Year Ended June 30, 1938-Date*. Knoxville, Tennessee: TVA. processed.

An explanation of TVA's relationship with the municipal electric departments and cooperatives purchasing its power, together with a balance sheet for each such purchaser. Also available in TVA *Annual Reports*.

FORESTRY AND WILDLIFE

Baker, Willis M. and Landess, W. M. Education for Sustained Regional Productivity. bibliog. *Journal of Educational Sociology.* 15:160-174, November 1941.

The methods and accomplishments of TVA's educational programs to combat forest fires, encourage tree planting, and to teach correct plowing and fertilizing.

Tennessee Valley Authority. *Forests and Human Welfare*. Washington: Government Printing Office, 1940. 46p.

A graphic presentation of how sustained forestry prevents soil erosion, improves crops, and generally benefits human welfare in the valley and the nation.

Fish

Eschmeyer, R. William and Tarzwell, C. M. Analysis of Fishing in the TVA Impoundments During 1939. *Journal of Wildlife Management,* 5:15-41, January 1941.

A summary of the creel census taken at Norris and Wheeler reservoirs and the tailwater area below Wilson Dam to serve as a basis for state regulations balancing the ratio of coarse to game fishes.

Tree Crops

Kline, Ludwig V. Tree Crops for the Tennessee Valley. *American Forests,* 47:470-472, October 1941.

Summary of trees studied as possible crops for the valley area, particularly the persimmon, black walnut, Asiatic chestnut, black and honey locust species.

HEALTH AND SAFETY

Bishop, Eugene L. The Health and Safety Services of the Tennessee Valley Authority. *Public Personnel Review*, 4:9-16, January 1943.
The organization and administration of the TVA Health and Safety Department with a description of the services performed.

Malaria Control

Tennessee Valley Authority. Health and Safety Department. *Malaria and Its Control in the Tennessee Valley*. 2d ed. Chattanooga, Tennessee: TVA, March 1942. 41p. bibliog. processed.
The basic facts concerning malaria: its cause, transmission, prevalence, and methods of control.

Stream Pollution

Tennessee Valley Authority. Health and Safety Department. *Studies of the Pollution of the Tennessee River System*, by G. R. Scott. Chattanooga, Tennessee: TVA, February 1941. 126p. processed.
Methods, results and conclusions of detailed studies of the pollution in the Tennessee River, measured at 24 stations near the four centers of population along the river, accompanied by maps and charts.

LABOR RELATIONS

Clapp, Gordon R. Problems of Union Relations in Public Agencies. *American Economic Review*, 33:sup 184-196, March 1943.
An examination and justification of collective bargaining in public employment, and a detailed picture of the growth and structure of labor relations in TVA.

King, Judson. *The TVA Labor Relations Policy at Work; Successful Cooperation Between Public Power and Organized Labor in the Public Interest*. Rev. ed. Washington: National Popular Government League, April 19, 1940. 64p. (Bulletin 192-A).
A review of labor-management relations in TVA, showing that collective bargaining by public employees may with sincere cooperation work advantageously to both. The TVA *Employee Relationship Policy* is reprinted in full.

LIBRARIES

Chancellor, John. *The Library in the TVA Adult Education Program.* Chicago: American Library Association, 1937. 75p.
The TVA library program as an example of a library-education organization which may prove to be a significant pattern in the future.

MANAGEMENT

Pritchett, C. Herman. *Tennessee Valley Authority; a Study in Public Administration.* Chapel Hill, North Carolina: University of North Carolina Press, 1943. 333p.
Major emphasis in this book is placed upon the administrative organization and achievements of the TVA. The author discusses the background of the TVA, its multiple-purpose program, and its historical development. A basic reference, liberally footnoted to a wide variety of source material.

MINERALS

Furcron, Aurelius S. and Teague, K. H. *Mica-Bearing Pegmatites of Georgia.* Atlanta, Georgia: Division of Conservation, 1943. 192p. bibliog. (Geological Survey. Bulletin No. 48).
Hunter, Charles E. *Forsterite Olivine Deposits of North Carolina and Georgia.* Raleigh, North Carolina: Division of Mineral Resources, 1941. 117p. (Bulletin No. 41).
Whitlatch, George I. *The Clays of West Tennessee.* Nashville, Tennessee: Division of Geology, 1940. 368p. bibliog. (Bulletin 49).

PERSONNEL ADMINISTRATION

Greene, Lee S. Personnel Administration in the Tennessee Valley Authority. *Journal of Politics,* 1:171-194, May 1939.
The policy covering recruitment, nepotism, promotions and transfers, duties, classification, service ratings, adjustment of grievances, and collective bargaining is discussed.
Tennessee Valley Authority. Personnel Department. *Personnel Administration in the Tennessee Valley Authority; Interpreting the Experience of Eight Years.* Knoxville, Tennessee: TVA, 1942. 61p. mimeo. (Management Services Report No. 1).

An outline of the organization of the Personnel Department, its methods of employment, placement, classification and compensation, including TVA's employee relationship policies.

Education

Seay, Maurice F., ed. *Adult Education a Part of a Total Educational Program; a Description of the Educational and Training Program of the Tennessee Valley Authority*. Lexington, Kentucky: University of Kentucky, 1938. 192p. (Kentucky. University. College of Education. Bureau of School Service. Bulletin 10, No. 4, June 1938).

Employee Training

Gant, George F. and Hart, Henry C. The TVA Program for Developing Personnel Staff Replacements. *Public Personnel Review*, 3:265-271, October 1942.

The method of recruiting for personnel staff vacancies and of training assistants is described.

McGlothlin, William J. Employee Training in TVA During Wartime Expansion. *Public Personnel Review*, 4:244-253, October 1943.

Methods employed to recruit and train TVA personnel at the start of the war. Apprentice training, central training schools, and classes for professional personnel are outlined.

REGIONAL DEVELOPMENT

Chase, Stuart. *Rich Land, Poor Land; a Study of Waste in the Natural Resources of America*. New York: McGraw-Hill Book Company, 1936. 361p. bibliog.

The author attempts to report the temper of the land and the outlook for its perpetuation. The efforts of the TVA to restore the land in the region in which it operates are described.

Hansen, Alvin H. and Perloff, Harvey S. *Regional Resource Development*. Washington: National Planning Association, 1942. 40p.

A post-war plan providing for conservation and expansion by regions, particularly in regard to water supply, land use, and power as exemplified by TVA.

TVA Program in Text and Pictures from the Architectural Forum; Reprinted from *Architectural Forum*, August 1939. Knoxville, Tennessee: TVA, 1939. 41p.

A graphic explanation of how the agriculture, industry, transportation, flood control and general prosperity of the valley are so interlocked as to benefit most from unified planning.

Community Planning

Augur, Tracy B. The Planning of the Town of Norris. *American Architect*, 148:18-26, April 1936.

The planning "from the ground up" of the town of Norris is outlined in detail, including house and community building plans.

Chapin, F. Stuart, Jr. *Communities for Living*. Prepared for the Advisory Panel on Regional Materials of Instruction for the Tennessee Valley. Athens, Georgia: University of Georgia Press, 1941. 56p.

An elementary study showing the need for community planning and its basic functions and principles.

Housing

Towne, Carroll A. Portable Housing. *New Pencil Points*, 23:49-56, July 1942.

Summary of TVA's experience in solving the low cost housing problem. One solution, the trailer house, is described in detail.

Local Government

Cooper, Weldon. *Municipal Government and Administration in Alabama*. University, Alabama: University of Alabama, 1940. 252p.

Municipal government in Alabama as of 1938-1939, showing typical forms of governmental administration, methods of finance, functions, and intergovernmental relations. Similar studies are available for Georgia, Mississippi, and Tennessee.

Durisch, Lawrence L. Local Government and the T.V.A. Program. *Public Administration Review*, 1:326-334, Summer 1941.

How TVA maintains "grass roots" contact with local governmental agencies. By establishing standards for its own employees in health, safety, education and other services, it has improved such services for those in surrounding areas. Cooperation with local governments described.

Tennessee Valley Authority. Department of Regional Studies. *County Government and Administration in the Tennessee Valley States*. Washington: Government Printing Office, 1940. 144p. bibliog.

This study outlines the organization and functions of the counties in the seven Tennessee Valley states.

Recreation

Tennessee Valley Authority. *Recreation Development of the Tennessee River System*. Washington: Government Printing Office, 1940. 99p. (76th Cong. H. Doc. 565).

A detailed study of recreation uses and development of TVA property, TVA promotion and assistance with state and local recreation, and the resulting benefits.

TVA Tax Payments

Durisch, Lawrence L. and Macon, Hershal L. Payments in Lieu of Taxes by the Tennessee Valley Authority. *Journal of Politics*, 3:318-334, August 1941.

Description in detail of the extensive payments being made by TVA to state and local governments, with examples of in lieu payment provisions of other federal agencies.

Edelmann, Alexander T. Public Ownership and Tax Replacements by the TVA. *American Political Science Review*, 35:727-737, August 1941.

A study of the payments made by TVA to various valley governmental units, in lieu of the taxes formerly collected by these units from the private utilities preceding TVA.

TRANSPORTATION RESEARCH

Freight Rates

Tennessee Valley Authority. *The Interterritorial Freight Rate Problem of the United States*. Washington: Government Printing Office, 1937. 66p. (75th Cong. H. Doc. 264).

The problem of discriminatory freight rates, particularly as they affect the South, is discussed as to structure and economic results, and possible solutions are suggested. Two additional TVA studies have been made of this problem:

Supplemental Phases of the Interterritorial Freight Rate Problem of the United States. Washington: Government Printing Office, 1939. 61p. (76th Cong. H. Doc. 271).

Regionalized Freight Rates: Barrier to National Productiveness. Washington: Government Printing Office, 1943. 79p. (78th Cong. H. Doc. 137).

Navigation

Tennessee Valley Authority. *A History of Navigation on the Tennessee River System; an Interpretation of the Economic Influence of this River System on the Tennessee Valley.* Washington: Government Printing Office, 1937. 192p. bibliog. (75th Cong. H. Doc. 254).

A detailed study of the navigational and economic importance of the river from 1701 to 1937.

Tennessee Valley Authority. Commerce Department. *Prospective Commerce on the Tennessee River.* Prepared by W. J. Sheehan. Knoxville, Tennessee: TVA, February 1941. 82p.

INDEX

Prepared by Sandford F. Brandt of the TVA staff